Built in Washington

Built in Washington

12,000 years of Pacific Northwest archaeological sites and historic buildings

Written by the Staff of the Washington State Office of Archaeology and Historic Preservation

Washington State Historical Society Tacoma, Washington
Washington State Office of Archaeology and Historic Preservation   Olympia, Washington
Washington State University Press Pullman, Washington
1989

Washington State University Press, Pullman, Washington 99164-5910
Printed in the United States of America.

First Edition.
99 98 97 96 95 94 93 92 91 90   10 9 8 7 6 5 4 3 2 1
Library of Congress Cataloging-in-Publication Data
Built in Washington: 12,000 years of Pacific Northwest archaeological sites and historic buildings / by Kay Austin . . .
[et al.]. p. cm. Includes bibliographical references.
1. Washington (State)–Antiquities. 2. Historic buildings–Washington (State). 3. Indians of North
America—Washington (State)—Antiquities. 4. Washington (State)–History, Local. I. Austin, Kay, 1951-.
     F893.B85 1989   979.7-- dc20   89-24823   ISBN 0-87422-065-3

Built in Washington was written by the staff of the Washington State Office of Archaeology and Historic Preservation,
Department of Community Development. Contributing authors were Kay Austin, Leonard Garfield, Greg Griffith,
David Hansen, Jake Thomas, and Rob Whitlam. Sara Steel served as the Project Coordinator; publication design by
Stone McLaren; and editorial supervision by WSU Press. Major funding for this book was provided by a grant from
the 1989 Washington Centennial Commission. Additional funding and support was provided by the Washington State
Historical Society and the Washington State University Press.

Cover illustration: "Mill Office for the Weyerhaeuser Timber Company," 1923, Bebb and Gould Architects, (Special
Collections Division, University of Washington).

Contents

Introduction

The purpose of this book is twofold: to create an awareness of the rich cultural heritage of our state, and to encourage recognition and preservation of this heritage.

The structures included here share several important characteristics. First, most are still standing and continue to provide powerful visual evidence of how earlier residents lived and worked. Furthermore, these structures survive in large part because concerned citizens refused to let them be demolished or fall into disrepair. Finally, almost all the properties mentioned here are listed in either the National Register or State Register of Historic Places.

Since 1966, the National Register of Historic Places has served as America's official honor roll of properties that best reflect the nation's history. In Washington state, over 1000 buildings, structures, sites, and districts have been added to this special list because of their historical or architectural significance. Listing in the National Register provides national recognition, insures legal protection when properties are affected by government projects, and makes financial assistance available for some rehabilitation projects. An additional 200 properties are listed in the Washington State Register, and over 20,000 properties are included in the State Inventory of Cultural Resources.

The National Register, State Register, and State Inventory are programs administered by the Washington State Office of Archaeology and Historic Preservation. This office is involved with many federal and state preservation programs, and is committed to identifying, preserving, and protecting cultural resources. It also is dedicated to serving those preservationists in Washington—the countless property owners, concerned neighbors, and local groups—who keep a vigilant watch over our historic sites.

It is our continuing responsibility to recognize the significance of Washington's irreplaceable cultural resources. We invite you to participate in their preservation and become stewards of our past.

Washington State Office of
Archaeology and Historic Preservation

HEARTH AREA:
CHARCOAL SAMPLE FROM HERE

POSSIBLE ENTRANCE AREA

Chapter One

1 METER

Ⓡ ROCK
S SHELL
• LITHIC FLAKE
▓ CHARCOAL/BURNED AREA

NOTE: HOUSEPIT BOUNDARY BASED UPON SOIL COLOR DIFFERENCES AND ARTIFACT DENSITY
JTS 7-23-84

Washington's First Builders

For thousands of years, Indian people have occupied the Washington landscape. Physical remnants of their lives from times long past—tools, evidences of dietary habits, artistic and practical fabrication efforts—are found across the state in archaeological sites. The scientific investigation of these sites, through the recovery and analysis of artifacts and cultural material, provides insight into Washington's prehistory. No other record presents the empirical evidence of the day-to-day life of our state's earliest peoples, or the environments in which they lived.

Archaeological sites abound in Washington, from the Pacific Coast, to the crest of the Cascade Range, to the Columbia Plateau of eastern Washington. Some are remnants of small temporary habitation sites in the mountains, prairies, or in protected caves; others constitute the remains of large permanent villages; still more are evidence of specialized hunting, fishing, plant gathering, rock quarrying, and artistic activities. Collectively, these sites combine to give testimony to the rich cultural heritage discoverable through archaeological research.

The Paleo-Indians

Current evidence indicates that Native Americans probably arrived in Washington over 12,000 years ago. It was a time of drastic environmental change, and the newcomers occupied a far different landscape from the one in which we live today. Glacial ice covered much of the Cascade Range and the Olympic Mountains, and the great Canadian ice shield had only recently withdrawn from the northern part of the state. The melting of the great glacial lobes exposed barren terrain that was quickly colonized by plant and animal life, some of which, such as mammoths and mastodons, now is extinct. A rise in sea level and changes in river courses also occurred as the great ice sheets melted. The scablands

of eastern Washington were created when, on several occasions, glacial ice dams broke in a western Montana valley, releasing catastrophic floods that scoured the Columbia basin lowlands. There also was volcanic activity during this period; Mt. St. Helens erupted 13,000, 12,000, and 8,700 years ago, and Glacier Peak spewed ash 11,250 years ago. Washington's current landscapes, shorelines, and rivers were, in some measure, molded by these massive forces of earth, fire, water, and ice.

Washington's original inhabitants were descendants, of unknown generations, of those first Asian peoples who entered North America via the Bering land bridge, or Beringia, which once connected Alaska to Kamchatka and Siberia. Beringia had formed as land in the North Pacific when vast amounts of the earth's water became locked in the great continental ice sheets, lowering sea levels worldwide. Since the end of the last ice age some 10,000 years ago, of course, Beringia has receded beneath the waves.

Termed "Paleo-Indians" by archaeologists, Washington's earliest people were mobile hunters entering the state either by coastal or interior routes. Over twenty sites are known from this early time. Most have been found in eastern Washington and include, for example, a winter occupation site in the Marmes Rockshelter on the

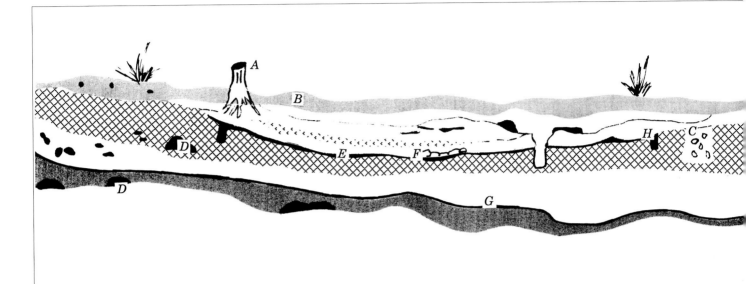

Stratigraphy

A stratigraphic profile is a "layer cake" view of a vertical section of earth which reflects different eras with associated cultural material. Different layers can be determined by changes in color, texture, and mixture of materials, and dates on individual strata can be determined by radiocarbon procedures or by association with geologic events such as volcanic eruptions or floods. The upper levels reveal the most recent history; lower layers are older. Seen here are (a) tree stump, (b) 500 year old soil deposit, (c) storage pit, (d) rocks, (e) compacted floor area of a 2000 year old housepit site, (f) cooking hearth, (g) volcanic ash from the Crater Lake eruption 6700 years ago, and (h) post mold.

Rock Alignment

Rock walls are found throughout the Columbia Plateau, usually in high rocky places with prominent views. They are thought to be features common at Native American sacred places associated with vision quests or other spiritual practices. Generally the walls are five- to eight-feet in length and two- to three-feet high. (State Inventory)

Storage Pit

Rock pits commonly were constructed for food storage by Indians on the Columbia Plateau, and were used to preserve winter provisions and emergency rations. After digging a hole approximately one-meter deep in loose rock, dried or prepared foodstuffs such as camas roots, berries, fish, or meat were placed in the hole and covered with large stones or cobbles. The loose rock covering the cache and the earthen pit provided air circulation, insulation, and a constant low temperature that helped preserve the contents. Pits were usually dug in late fall, within close proximity of a village, and were left unmarked to prevent pilferage. (State Inventory)

Palouse River, a frequently used fishery at Kettle Falls, a hunting and hide processing area at Lind Coulee in Grant County, a seasonally used seed and vegetal processing camp at Goldendale, and a cache of unusual stone projectile points in an East Wenatchee apple orchard.

Paleo-Indians had a distinctive stone tool technology and crafted sophisticated projectile points for spears and darts. Crescent-shaped knives, choppers, bola stones, manos, net sinkers, milling stones, scrapers, and burins also were utilized. Animal remains found at Paleo-Indian sites are predominantly from large game—prehistoric bison, deer, elk, and antelope—though a wide variety of smaller animals also were hunted.

In western Washington, one of the most intriguing discoveries yet made is located on the Manis property near Sequim in Clallam County, which has been described as a possible mastodon kill site. Archaeologists, however, found few of the lithic materials that characteristically have been uncovered at other Paleo-Indian excavations, and stone projectile points, in particular, apparently were absent. On the other hand, a single, pointed splinter of bone was found embedded in one of the mastodon's ribs, reputedly the result of a spear or dart thrust. The rib showed signs of healing around the imbedded point, indicating that the wound was not fatal and the ice-age elephant escaped; it did die from other causes sometime later. The presence of this bone point, as well as the physical displacement of the individual bones of the skeleton, have been attributed to human action. Radiocarbon dating of the site yielded an age of 11,850 years ago. If this is a Paleo-Indian site, it is the earliest known occupation in western Washington, and may reflect the movement of people into coastal areas as the glaciers melted.

In eastern Washington, the recent discovery of a cache of ancient stone tools in the Richey-Roberts orchard at East Wenatchee has yielded the largest Paleo-Indian Clovis points ever found in the United States or elsewhere. Some of the beautifully crafted points are over eight- and one-half-inches long; they may have been used as ceremonial objects. This trove of over thirty artifacts, dating from over 11,000 years ago, promises to provide exciting new insights about the earliest Americans.

Peoples of the Interior

Over succeeding millennia, the evolving climate gradually became similar to what we are accustomed to living in today. The changing environmental conditions, of course, continued to shape the lives of the Native American

**Indian Boys
Building a House**

As the white population of Washington grew, the native peoples were encouraged to abandon most of their traditional beliefs and practices. On the coast, Indian agents and missionaries forced them to tear down their old houses, and rebuild with more modern techniques and tools. Old villages on Indian reservations were platted in square blocks, with streets laid out at right angles. In this circa 1889 photo, a group of Indian boys at a reservation school demonstrate their proficiency with the white man's tools. The outside shape of the building on which they are working meets the newly imposed standards, but the internal supports reflect their own traditional building techniques.

Mat Lodge
Commonly a winter dwelling in eastern Washington, mat lodges were built of pole frames in the shape of an "inverted-V" covered with woven tule mats or bark. An opening was left along the ridgepole for smoke to escape. The larger lodges were as high as twenty-feet, twenty- to forty-feet long, and ten- to fifteen-feet across, with a row of hearths down the center. Constructed in an oblong shape, the lodge could have door openings at one or both ends and could accommodate multiple families.

inhabitants. In eastern Washington, a multitude of resources, most notably the abundant salmon fisheries of the Columbia and Snake watersheds, provided the economic basis for a diversity of Native American cultures. These people had extensive trade networks, occupied large villages, and developed complex mythologies and value systems.

A cultural mosaic reflecting varying local responses to specific environmental circumstances became evident during this period. Archaeology has revealed less emphasis upon hunting large game, and an increased reliance on fish, particularly salmon. Other resources, such as river

mussels, small mammals, birds, and a very extensive use of plant foods, complemented the fisheries.

The vast technology utilized in exploiting and processing these diverse resources has been clearly indicated by the wide variety of tools uncovered in archaeological sites. For example, chipped stone artifacts have been found, including small corner, side, and base notched projectile points, which suggest the use of the bow and arrow. Stone also was ground into net weights, pestles, grinding stones, and mortars, and large river cobbles were chipped to form chopping tools. Wood and fiber were utilized to make mats, cordage, awls, firestarters, and arrow foreshafts. Items made from bone and shell included awls, needles, projectile points, beads, and pendants.

Reliance on natural resources resulted in a settlement and subsistence pattern that shifted through the year. As the seasons turned, Native Americans traveled about to take advantage of indigenous foodstuffs. The cyclical movement to spring root collecting camps, to summer fishing stations, to early fall berry picking sites, to fall hunting camps, and to sheltered winter villages was a Plateau pattern that is clearly revealed in the archaeological record. Excavations suggest that this basic lifestyle may have been established as early as 6,500 years ago, and continued up until recent centuries. In fact, the first European and American explorers encountered Native Americans practicing this specialized utilization of local resources.

Archaeological investigations at winter village sites, such as those excavated in the Chief Joseph, Wells, and Rock Island reservoirs on the Columbia River, have produced much evidence about Native American construction methods. Two basic types of prehistoric houses were used in eastern Washington—those partially dug into the earth (pithouses), and others that were built entirely aboveground (longhouses, or mat lodges). The pithouse may represent one of the oldest indigenous forms of Native American architecture. Pithouses normally were circular in shape, with an excavated living space about three-feet below the outside ground surface. The structures ranged from ten- to thirty-feet in diameter, and featured a central fire hearth. The roof consisted of a pole framework covered with matting, logs, or bark, which was covered over with a layer of earth. The entrance was in the side or through the roof. Pithouses were well suited for eastern Washington's cold winters and hot summers.

The longhouse, or mat lodge, was another important type of structure east of the Cascades, particularly in the

Indian Fort
This early sketch by artist Joseph Drayton, entitled "Sachet Stronghold; Whidby's Island," demonstrates that the Indians built forts on the frontier long before white settlers arrived. Generally, these palisades offered protection from aggressive northern coastal tribes.

Peeled Cedar Tree
The western red cedar was an especially important source of basic materials for Washington's coastal Indians. Every part of the tree was used. Cedar logs were carved into canoes or used to build shelters and long-houses. Bark was peeled from the trees, as shown in this photograph, and used for many purposes. Indian women wove strips of cedar bark into baskets and mats, or twined it into cordage to make ropes and waterproof containers. It was woven into garments, even diapers for babies. And, for berry gathering, folded pieces of cedar bark stitched at the sides formed baskets. The inner bark contains a natural preservative that helps preserve the berries for many months. (State Inventory)

more recent prehistoric era. These "A" frame shaped structures, standing entirely aboveground, consisted of pole supports covered with woven reed mats or bark. They usually ranged in size from twenty- to forty-feet long and ten- to fifteen-feet across. The larger lodges, housing several families, had multiple entrances and a row of hearths down the center.

Excavations at Kettle Falls, The Dalles, and other ancient fisheries have provided important information about prehistoric fishing techniques and structures. Most notable were the intricate platforms and weirs at river rapids that allowed Indian fishermen to net and spear migrating salmon. Similarly, archaeological research near Usk in the northeast corner of Washington has provided extensive data about prehistoric root gathering and vegetable processing methods. The most important finds there were the innumerable large earth ovens that Native Americans constructed to cook vast quantities of camas bulbs harvested from wet meadows in the springtime. The ovens were circular earthen pits lined with fire-heated rocks; the camas was steam heated under a covering of ferns, skunk cabbage, bark, and earth or sand. Camas and other naturally occurring roots have long been important staples in the Plateau Indian diet.

In addition, hunting blinds, rock alignments, and artistic drawings and carvings (termed pictographs and petroglyphs) are found along the basaltic outcrops and cliffs of central and eastern Washington; they remain as silent testimony of times long past.

Peoples of the Coast

Temperate zone meadows and forests, along with rich marine resources, provided the economic base which enabled Washington's coastal peoples to develop large permanent villages, an extensive artistic tradition, intricate social structures, and elaborate mythologies that were unsurpassed by any preagricultural societies anywhere in the world. Northwest Coast seagoing hunters and shoreline gatherers were the exception to the accepted scientific belief that the adoption of agriculture (i.e., farming) was a prerequisite for the creation of large permanent villages, a ranked social hierarchy, and monumental architecture. These people were able to literally "harvest" a rich bounty of natural food resources from the sea and coast, leaving much time for extensive cultural and artistic development.

Native Americans west of the Cascades developed a mosaic of adaptations to local environmental conditions, in this case in a temperate maritime climate. The people of Washington's coasts and waterways were skilled fishermen, hunters, and plant collectors, who relied upon naturally recurring seasonal foodstuffs, such as salmon and other fish, marine mammals and birds, shellfish, and berries, roots, and other vegetal resources.

Coastal peoples were adept artisans, producing a great variety of tools and other items from stone, bone, wood, and plants. Their maritime orientation was reflected in the wide range of harpoons, nets, and other elaborate fishing equipment that they used. Northwest Coast peoples were especially noted for their skilled woodworking; by utilizing western red cedar in particular, they constructed bent-corner wooden boxes, large ocean-going canoes, and numerous other items and equipment, including their large plank houses with carved houseposts. The bark of the cedar tree likewise was used, and woven or twisted to produce baskets, cordage, nets, and garments.

Like most hunting and gathering societies, coastal peoples had a settlement and subsistence pattern based on a permanent winter village; from there a cycle of movements to smaller temporary camps was made to exploit locally available resources at different times of the year. Excavations and research at the Duwamish site in Seattle, Old Man House at Suquamish, and at Ozette on the Olympic Peninsula have revealed important information about what life was like in a winter village. The plank houses that they occupied consisted of a frame of upright and horizontal logs grooved to fit together. Cedar planks were lashed or fastened to these beams, forming walls and roofs. The interior of the houses could be divided into separate compartments for different families; a family's location within the house was an indication of social standing. Some structures were hundreds of feet long, and many had elaborate mythological figures and family crests carved and painted on the walls and structural supports. Individual houses even could have a distinct name and identity.

Archaeological work, such as at the Chester Morse Reservoir and Tokul Creek in King County, has provided information on seasonal hunting and fishing camps in the foothills of the Cascade Range. Radiocarbon dating from the Chester Morse project suggests that the area was utilized by Native Americans for thousands of years. Perhaps most spectacular, however, are the water saturated sites located on Puget Sound at Fishtown in Skagit County and at Ozette and the Hoko River on the Olympic Peninsula. These sites contain innumerable perishable wooden and fiber artifacts that are not normally preserved. Research at these locations has revealed the rich cultural heritage of the past, and the great skill with which prehistoric artisans fashioned not only tools, weavings, and other objects, but also the large elaborate plank houses that they occupied.

Ozette Village

The archaeological excavation of a Makah Indian village at Ozette provided valuable knowledge about the life and culture of Washington's early coastal residents. The longhouses in this winter village were typically framed with upright and horizontal logs grooved to fit together. Cedar planks were lashed or fastened to this frame, forming walls and the roof. Interior space was divided into separate compartments for families. This early 1900s photograph shows a transition from the early shed roof houses to ones with gable roofs. (National Register)

ALEXANDER BLO

COUPEVILLE,   WAS

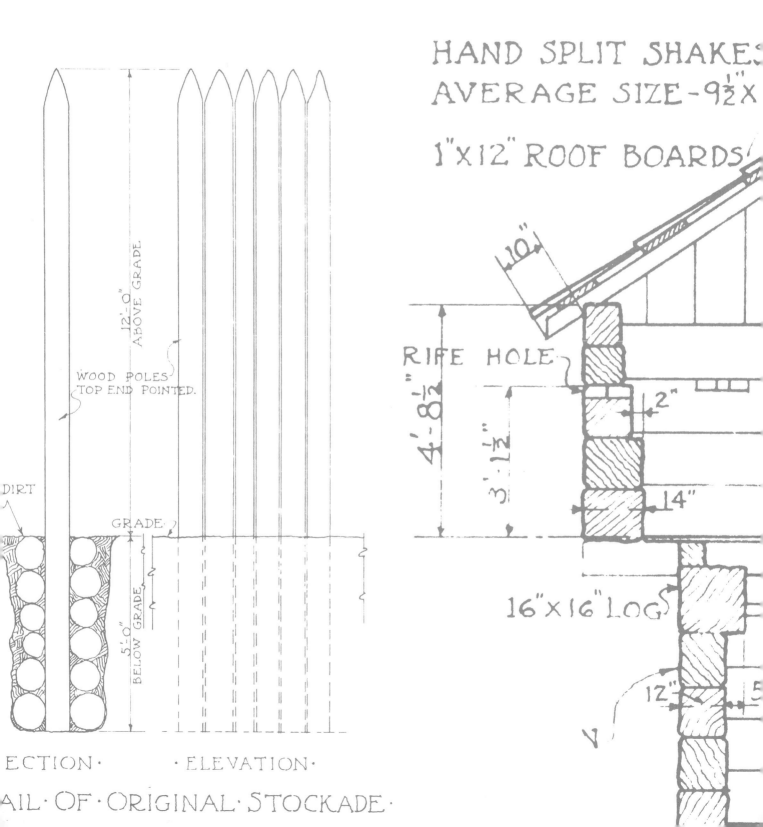

HAND SPLIT SHAKES
AVERAGE SIZE - 9½" X

1"x12" ROOF BOARDS

10"

RIFE HOLE

4'-8½"

3'-1½"

2"

14"

16"x16" LOG

12"

12'-0" ABOVE GRADE

WOOD POLES TOP END POINTED.

DIRT

GRADE

5'-0" BELOW GRADE

· ECTION ·   · ELEVATION ·

·AIL · OF · ORIGINAL · STOCKADE ·

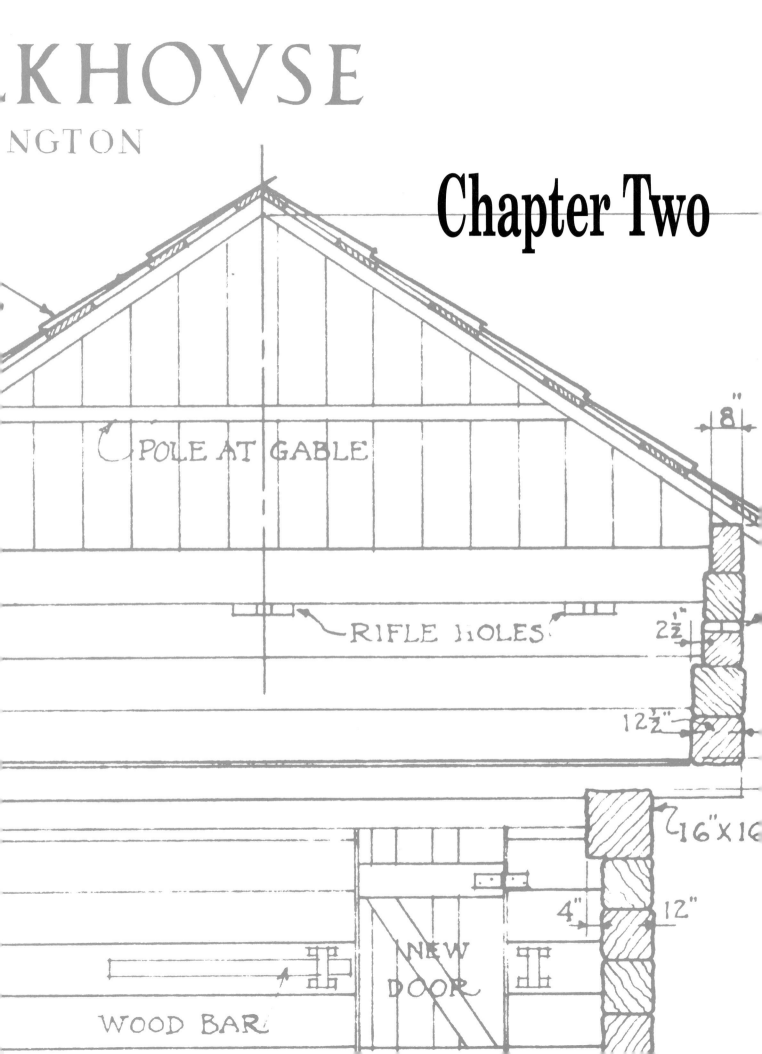

KHOVSE

NGTON

Chapter Two

8"

U POLE AT GABLE

RIFLE HOLES

2½"

12½"

16"X16

4" 12"

NEW DOOR

WOOD BAR

Buildings of the Early Frontier

When seagoing European explorers first plied the coastal waters of the Pacific Northwest, they searched for a "Northwest Passage" of myth and legend, as well as new lands to claim for the sake of empire. European maritime trading powers, particularly Great Britain, were eager to discover a route that would shorten the interminable voyage to China and the riches of the Orient. There had been persistent, but unfounded, rumors that a great waterway linking the Atlantic and Pacific oceans crossed through the largely unexplored northerly latitudes of the North American continent. No such waterway actually existed,

Crockett Blockhouse

In the 1840s and 1850s as the white population of Washington increased rapidly, Native Americans became increasingly suspicious and hostile toward the settlers. Warfare broke out in 1855 in eastern Washington, and the following year west of the Cascades. White families who lived near fortified posts sought shelter in blockhouses and bastions built by soldiers and local militia groups. Some of these remain intact, including the Crockett blockhouse, one of three still standing on Whidbey Island. Erected in 1855 of square-hewn logs, it is typical of blockhouse construction. Small loopholes in the upper story were intended to serve as gun sites and widely spaced floorboards in the overhang allowed defenders to fire down on unsuspecting attackers. The Whidbey Island blockhouses and Fort Borst near Centralia are silent monuments from a hostile era. (National Register)

Grant House

Completed about 1851 as part of Vancouver Barracks, the Grant house is named in honor of Ulysses S. Grant, who served as Post Quartermaster in 1852-1853. Originally built of logs, the structure was remodelled in 1885, at which time the wooden siding and elegant porches were added. (National Register)

of course, but the search for the fictitious "Northwest Passage," in addition to imperial ambitions and scientific inquisitiveness, led to the exploration of the Pacific Northwest.

In the last quarter of the eighteenth century, Spanish, British, and American seafarers thoroughly charted the Northwest Coast. Though not finding a channel through the continent, they stumbled on an unexpected source of great wealth; sea otter and

other valuable fur-bearing animals were plentiful along the coast. Upon visiting China, British naval explorers quickly learned that furs of all types, but particularly the almost iridescent pelt of the sea otter, were in great demand in Macao and Canton.

Consequently, in the 1780s scores of merchant vessels from Europe, the United States, and Latin America began putting in at sheltered bays along the North Pacific coast to barter trade items for furs from the indigenous people. In China, the pelts were exchanged for tea, cloth, and other fine goods, which in turn brought substantial profits in the European and American markets.

The lucrative maritime fur trade, however, sharply increased tension between two old antagonists— Spain and Great Britain. The two European colonial powers disagreed about the nature of their mutual presence in the Pacific Northwest: Spain asserted an imperial claim to the North Pacific coast, while Great Britain demanded. increased commercial rights.

The matter came to a head at Nootka Sound on Vancouver Island in 1789, when a Spanish officer arrested some British seafarers and took them back to Mexico in irons. Officials in the highest echelons of the British and Spanish governments quickly were drawn into the dispute. Years of lengthy diplomatic discussion followed before a resolution was reached, resulting in a weakening of Spanish claims while Great Britain was allowed a greater opportunity to develop trade and occupy the region.

During the ongoing international dispute, Spanish authorities established the first European settlement in what is now Washington in an attempt to strengthen Spain's claim to the region. Named Nunez Gaona, the small, palisaded village stood on the tip of the Olympic Peninsula. It was abandoned after a short time, however, when the commander, Salvador Fidalgo, was ordered to proceed to another temporary Spanish base at Nootka Sound on Vancouver Island.

Continental Fur Trade, 1805-1846

As it became clear that no great waterway, or "Northwest Passage," flowed through the continent, interest shifted to finding the most direct routes by land to the Pacific Northwest. The driving forces behind these efforts remained the fur trade and Oriental commerce, national and imperial ambitions, and scientific and geographical inquiry.

In the first decade of the nineteenth century, the U. S. Army's Lewis and Clark Expedition and David Thompson of Canada's North West Company forged new trails to the Pacific Northwest. Canadian and American fur hunters quickly followed in their footsteps, establishing fortified trading posts in the region to barter furs from the Indians.

In 1810 or 1811, Finan McDonald and Jacques Finlay, Canadian employees of the North West Company, built Spokane House at the junction of the Spokane and Little Spokane rivers. Other trading posts soon were erected in what is now Washington, including Fort Okanogan (1811), Fort Walla Walla (1818), Fort Colvile (1825), and Fort Vancouver (1825).

By the 1820s, however, British traders of the Hudson's Bay Company (HBC) overcame all American and Canadian rivals, emerging as the Northwest's dominant commercial enterprise. Fort Vancouver was the headquarters for the HBC's widely scattered posts in the Columbia Department, which extended from the Russian settlements in the north to Spanish California in the south, and from the Pacific Ocean to the crest of the Rocky Mountains.

In addition to the forts located east of the Cascades, two other supporting outposts were established in the 1830s in what is now western Washington; these included Cowlitz Landing (near present-day Toledo in Lewis County) and Fort Nisqually (located on Puget

Sound near today's DuPont). Smaller British controlled facilities and farms eventually were established on San Juan Island and at other locations as well. HBC trading posts, with their British, French Canadian, Hawaiian (brought in by supply ships), and mixed breed occupants, formed the core of Washington's first permanent non-Indian settlements, particularly at Fort Vancouver and Cowlitz Landing.

As the fur trade waned in the late 1830s, the British expanded their activities to include lumbering and agriculture in order to maintain profits and strengthen Great Britain's claim to the region. These facilities supplied and succored not only Washington's early Canadian and local Indian inhabitants, but also American immigrants who began arriving in ever increasing numbers by the early 1840s.

Today, it is fortunate indeed that two especially noteworthy structures from the HBC's Fort Nisqually still stand, though they have been relocated in Tacoma's Point Defiance Park many miles from their original location. These important buildings include the old Fort Nisqually granary, built in approximately 1843 and believed to be the oldest remaining intact structure in the state, and the chief factor's house, dating from a few years later. Both exhibit important architectural features characteristic of buildings erected by Canadians on the frontier.

The granary, in particular, was built in the distinctive Red River style, whereby square-hewn wall timbers were laid horizontal one on top of the other, and fastened at the ends, in tongue and groove fashion, by vertical support beams.

Protestant missionaries arrived a little more than a decade after the Hudson's Bay Company consolidated fur trading activities in the Pacific Northwest. Catholic priests followed shortly thereafter. Whereas the HBC strived to maintain traditional Native American lifeways for the benefit of the fur trade, most missionaries intended to institute drastic changes in tribal life. They saw the Indians as a collection of souls to be civilized and converted to Christianity, and the Protestants, in particular, wanted to change these free-roaming native peoples into sedentary farmers.

Marcus and Narcissa Whitman were the first missionaries in Washington, arriving in 1836 to establish the Waiilatpu mission in the Walla Walla Valley and proselytize among the Cayuse and neighboring tribes. Other missionaries soon followed both east and west of the Cascades.

Over the next ten years, the Whitman's expanded their facilities at Waiilatpu to serve as a school, hospital, and provisioning center not only for

Native Americans, but also for white immigrants who passed by in increasing numbers. By the 1840s, in fact, the Whitmans and other Protestant missionaries actively began to encourage and support white colonization. During this period, Catholic priests established their own mission stations at Cowlitz Landing, Nisqually, Okanogan, Colvile, St. Ignatius (near Usk on the Pend Oreille River), and St. Joseph's (in the Yakima country).

The Whitmans met a tragic end when the Waiilatpu mission was destroyed by disillusioned and disgruntled elements of the Cayuse tribe in November 1847. In the following conflict between the Cayuse and Oregon territorial militia troops (1847-1850), other Protestant missions east of the Cascades were abandoned, though the Catholic priests managed to maintain a foothold in the interior. Following the cessation of the Cayuse war, the Catholics resumed their activities east of the Cascades, whereas the Protestants remained largely absent in following decades.

Today, nearly all of the old mission buildings from the pioneer era are gone, but one particularly noteworthy survivor is the 1867 Catholic log structure at St. Joseph's mission on Ahtanum Creek in the Yakima vicinity. Another excellent example of Catholic mission architecture is St. Paul's log

chapel at Kettle Falls on the upper Columbia. It is largely rebuilt, however, and has been moved to high ground from its original location at the HBC's Fort Colvile site, which was inundated after 1941 with the completion of Grand Coulee Dam and the impounding of the Franklin D. Roosevelt Reservoir.

Territorial Era, 1846-1889

The earliest American immigrants, coming west in the 1830s and early 1840s via the Oregon Trail or on seagoing vessels, settled in the Willamette Valley in what is now Oregon. At the time, the Hudson's Bay Company

Nathaniel Orr Home
Nathaniel Orr arrived in what is now Steilacoom in 1852, and was one of the first white settlers to build with locally milled lumber. A wagonmaker and orchardist, Orr planted the grounds surrounding his homesite with fruit trees, some of which remain productive today. The wagon shop also is intact, and several of the family's original furnishings decorate the home. (National Register)

Fort Nisqually

Fort Nisqually was one of the noteworthy trading posts established by the Hudson's Bay Company in the 1820s and 1830s. There were, in fact, two Fort Nisquallys built by the HBC and the Puget's Sound Agricultural Company near the present-day town of DuPont. The first, constructed in 1833, was a small outpost surrounded by a palisade. In 1843, this settlement was relocated to a nearby prairie with a more reliable water supply. This site later was included within DuPont's explosives manufacturing complex. In the 1930s, a couple of the buildings from the second Fort Nisqually were moved to Tacoma's Point Defiance Park by the Young Men's Business Club. These included the granary and the chief factor's house. The granary is an outstanding example of the HBC's distinctive Red River building style, in which square-hewn wall planks were stacked horizontally, and fastened tongue and groove fashion into vertical corner posts. (Granary, National Register and National Historic Landmark)

Olmstead Place

One of the original white settlers in the Kittitas Valley, Samuel Bedient Olmstead brought his family to Washington Territory from Connecticut. This cabin, built of square-hewn cottonwood logs, joined with dovetail notches, was constructed in 1875. Other intact structures on the homestead include a dairy barn built in 1892, and a wagon shed erected in 1894. (National Register)

hoped to hold the area north of the Columbia River under British control and keep Americans out. In the mid 1840s, however, American settlers started pushing northward into what is now western Washington. According to the terms of the 1819 joint occupation agreement, both British and American citizens could move freely throughout the area.

The influx of large numbers of American immigrants inevitably led to a resolution of the "Oregon Question." In 1846, British and American diplomats established the international boundary at the 49th parallel, dividing the "Oregon Country" into British possessions to the north (today's British Columbia) and American territory to the south (now Washington, Idaho, Oregon, and parts of western Montana and Wyoming). In 1848, the U. S. Congress designated the entire American sector as Oregon Territory; then, in 1853, established a separate Washington Territory (it originally included what is now Washington, northern Idaho, and Montana west of the continental divide).

During this period, of course, most settlers built hand-hewn log cabins in the wilderness with axe, saw, and broadax. Milled lumber, on the other hand, was less utilized; the relatively few water-powered sawmills of the day were inaccessible to many immigrants or produced lumber that was too costly. Cheap lumber turned out by steam-powered sawmills was still about two decades away.

Both square-hewed and round logs were utilized in pioneer construction. Some good examples of log houses remaining today from the frontier era in western Washington include the John R. Jackson cabin (north of Toledo, 1845), which is probably Washington's oldest standing house, and the O. B. McFadden cabin (Chehalis, 1859), the home of an early territorial judge. The Perkins cabin in Colfax, built by an early town developer, and the Olmstead Place cabin near Ellensburg, owned by one of the Kittitas Valley's earliest settlers, both date from the 1870s and document early settlement east of the Cascades.

Interestingly enough, some of the state's oldest surviving houses, such as the Nathaniel Orr home (Steilacoom, 1853), the George Pickett house (Bellingham, 1856), and the Joseph Borst home (Centralia, 1857), were built with milled lumber and other manufactured materials, rather than with logs. These were elaborate buildings for a frontier area, and were constructed only where sawmills were relatively close at hand, and, even then, much of the materials had to be imported. The window sashes of the Borst house, for example, were shipped

Commandant's Quarters at Fort Simcoe

Fort Simcoe, located southwest of Yakima, is an outstanding example of a U. S. Army post of the early territorial period. Established in 1856, and occupied by the Army until 1859, the post still includes Gothic style structures based on drawings in Andrew Jackson Downing's *The Architecture of Country Houses*. These are some of the oldest and least altered of any remaining frontier buildings in Washington. (National Register)

by sea from San Francisco, and the bricks used in erecting the T. G. Richards store (Bellingham, 1858) reputedly came from Philadelphia.

In this era, most Native Americans viewed white immigration with suspicion and, understandably, they were uncertain or troubled about treaties signed in the years 1854-1855. Warfare finally broke out east of the Cascades in late 1855, resulting in a series of military campaigns by U. S. Army and territorial militia units against Yakima, Klickitat, Palouse, and other allied Plateau tribesmen. Miners and stockmen in eastern Washington fled westward to the settlements on Puget Sound and the lower Columbia, though some gold miners remained in the Fort Colvile locality.

Generally known as the Yakima war, the conflict was destined to last three long years. While most of the male civilian population organized into local militia companies, the federal government sent additional troops to garrison posts in the region.

In early 1856, Yakima and Klickitat warriors crossed through the Cascade Range to join coastal Indian allies in attacks on American settlers. In the Puget Sound country, cabins were burned, crops destroyed, and livestock driven off. Full-scale Indian assaults were repulsed at the Cascades in the Columbia River gorge, and at Seattle, where defenders were aided by the *USS Decatur* anchored in Elliott Bay.

After several defeats, Indian hostility died down west of the Cascades, although Indian marauders from British Columbia remained a threat along the Puget Sound coast. These northern Indian raids were unrelated to the Indian war then taking place in Washington. For decades, in fact, the warlike Haidas and other northerly tribesmen had swept southward in their large seagoing canoes seeking booty and slaves in attacks on western Washington Indians, who themselves built fortifications for defense. American settlers were not exempt from Haida hostility either.

During the Indian wars, practically the entire white population of western Washington resided, at night at least, in stockaded settlements, or fortified bastions and cabins. Legacies of this period are the heavily timbered blockhouses that sheltered settlers. Some still remain intact at several locations. Three blockhouses, for example, stand on Whidbey Island in the Coupeville vicinity, and the stout "Fort Borst" blockhouse at Centralia has been refurbished; today it sits several thousand feet from its original location near the confluence of the Skookumchuck and Chehalis rivers.

By late 1856, the main focus of the conflict shifted to the rolling, grassy hills of the Columbia Plateau, where the U. S. Army, by adopting a largely nonbelligerent policy, temporarily quieted the warring tribes. Meanwhile, the Army angered territorial officials by banning white settlement east of the Cascades.

Hostilities flared up again, however, when Lieutenant Colonel Edward J. Steptoe's command of 150 troops barely escaped annihilation at the hands of Spokane, Palouse, Coeur d'Alene, and allied warriors near Rosalia in May 1858. That autumn, Colonel George Wright and a large force of regulars decisively defeated these tribes at Four Lakes and Spokane Plains, concluding Washington's last significant Indian campaign.

Military posts, of course, were focal points of settlement in territorial times, and fledgling communities often grew up in their protective shadows. Today, several excellent examples of frontier Army posts remain in Washington. In particular, Vancouver Barracks (established in 1849), Fort Steilacoom (founded 1849), Fort Walla Walla (dating from 1856), and Fort Simcoe (established 1856) are well preserved and, as such, represent the oldest and least altered of any original frontier building complexes dating from the territorial era.

Particularly noteworthy is Fort Simcoe, built and occupied by the U. S.

Army (1856-1859) and afterward turned into an Indian agency, and now preserved as Fort Simcoe State Park. At this location, a blockhouse and several officers' quarters remain in authentic and unaltered condition. These structures, along with several other carefully executed reconstructions of post buildings, present an especially authentic depiction of a U. S. Army post of the early territorial period.

From the 1850s through the 1870s, a typical community west of the Cascades consisted of a tiny cluster of frame and log buildings, which usually stood alongside a boat landing on a river or bay, since waterways were a primary means of transportation in the territorial era. Invariably, town fathers, boosters, and newspaper editors espoused great optimism for the future of their fledgling community, which they envisioned as someday becoming another "Chicago" or "New York" standing in the wilderness. Free town lots frequently were offered to those who would settle and live in the community, and even more inducements could be granted to anyone starting a business within the town's stump-strewn boundaries.

Ambition was in the driver's seat, and grand schemes, no matter how unrealistic, needed little more incentive to take shape than simple desire. Real, sustained growth, however, came with the railroads in the 1880s, after which time Tacoma, Seattle, Everett, and other communities grew at phenomenal rates.

Towns took shape later east of the mountains, with the notable exception of Walla Walla, which had been established adjacent to the U. S. Army's Fort Walla Walla in the late 1850s. In the 1860s, the great gold stampedes to Idaho, Montana, Oregon, and interior British Columbia ensured Walla Walla's future as an important regional transportation hub and commercial center. For a while, Walla Walla, with its large population and wealth, was the premier city of Washington Territory. Other eastern Washington communities grew rapidly during the 1880s, due to the influence of mining, agriculture, and railroads, with Spokane especially benefiting from that combination.

Today, in most Washington cities few or none of the original wooden commercial buildings erected in the territorial era still remain; typically, they were casually built and have not withstood the vicissitudes of time, especially fires. In the late nineteenth century, in particular, conflagrations swept through the business districts of practically every community in Washington, and often not just once, but on two or more occasions. Some communities never recovered from these setbacks.

The year of statehood, 1889, was especially disastrous as great holocausts burned out the heart of Seattle, Ellensburg, Spokane, and several other communities, razing practically all evidence of earlier generations of commercial buildings. By the 1890s, business districts in these cities were being reconstructed in brick and stone, reflecting the greater wealth of the times and a greater concern on the part of the builders for permanence and safety.

Joseph Borst Home
The Joseph Borst home, completed in 1857 near Centralia in the Greek Revival style, is a good example of box construction. The home featured locally milled lumber, a fireplace constructed from sandstone quarried in Tenino, and windows shipped from San Francisco. Great attention was paid to stylistic refinements— a typical urge of the pioneers to introduce elements of civilization and stability in the rough frontier environment. (National Register)

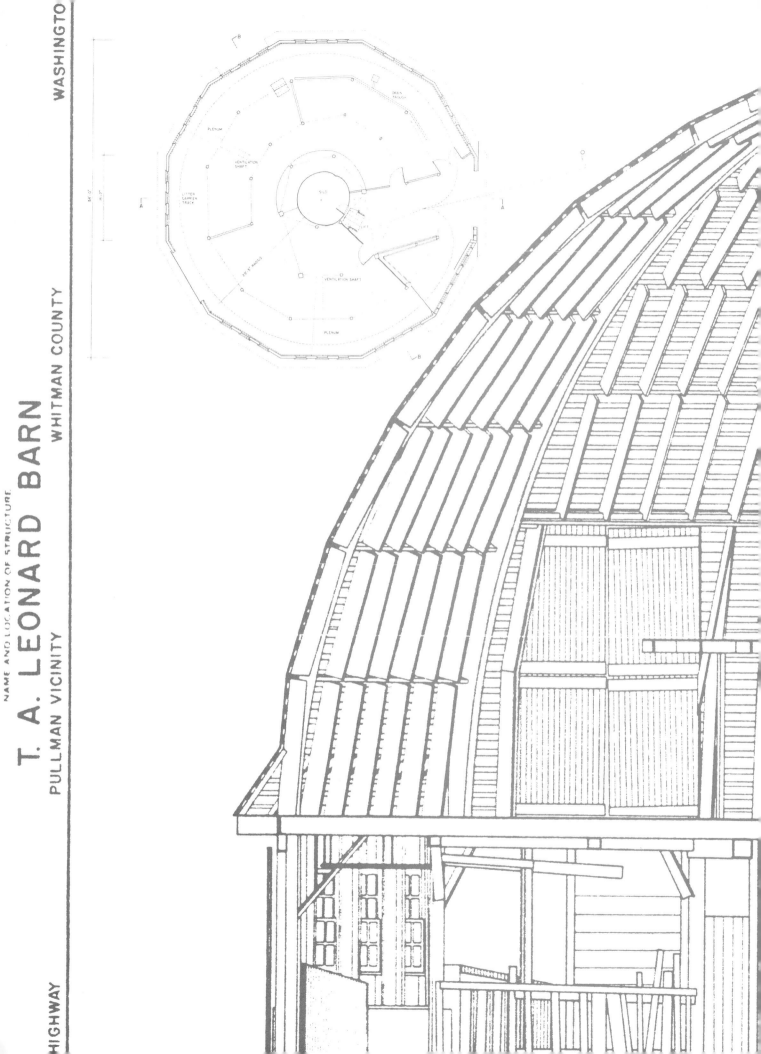

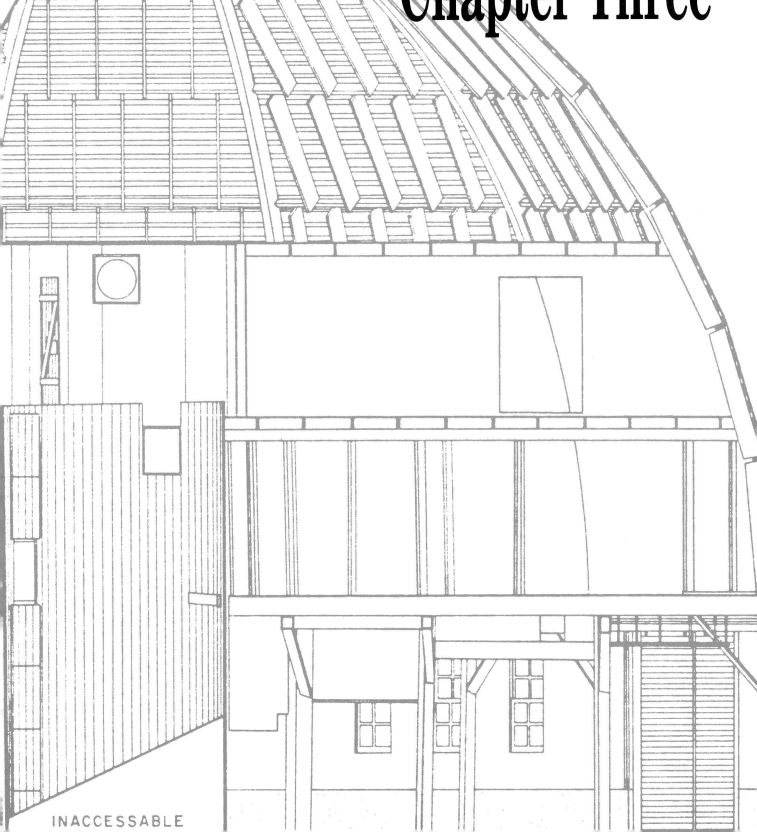

Chapter Three

INACCESSABLE

Bountiful Harvests

Agriculture has exerted a profound impact on Washington's population and landscape virtually from the earliest phases of settlement. In 1792, the Spanish at their short-lived colony on Neah Bay kept the region's first gardens, cattle, sheep, goats, and poultry. Two decades later, American and British fur hunters likewise planted crops at newly established trading posts. By the 1820s, the Hudson's Bay Company was raising grain, vegetables, fruit, hogs, and cattle at Fort Vancouver, Fort Colvile, Fort Walla Walla, and other locations both east and west of the Cascades to sustain company personnel and their families.

Marble Ranch Round Barn

As agriculture became increasingly important in the economy of Washington in the late nineteenth and early twentieth centuries, millions of acres were turned into wheat fields, fruit orchards, and livestock ranches. Closer to cities, small, independent truck farms and dairies flourished, providing fresh produce and milk products to a growing urban population. A few farmers experimented with a specialized barn design that had originated in the Midwest. Round barns were thought to be more efficient for sheltering, feeding, and milking cattle. The round shape of the structure was said to "take advantage of a cow's wedge-shaped anatomy," and the central feeding station would streamline both feed storage and cleanup. Few of these structures were built in Washington, however. Not only was there a lack of expertise in construction techniques, but also it became obvious that round barns were more expensive to build and maintain and could not be enlarged or expanded. The Marble Ranch round barn, south of Grandview in Yakima County, was built circa 1912-1916 by S. D. Cornell, a local dairy farmer. It was later sold to John Marble, one of the leading iris growers in the area.
(National Register)

Jacob Ebey House
Built in 1855 on property acquired through the Donation Land Law, Jacob Ebey's house is a fine example of a pioneer residence in terms of design, materials, and type of construction. The roofline is typical, as are the centered front entry, window arrangements, shiplap siding, and the vertical corner boards. (National Register)

By 1839, a group of HBC men formed the Puget's Sound Agricultural Company in an attempt to expand beyond subsistence farming and develop a system of export agriculture. They intended to ship farm products to Russian Alaska, California, England, and the Sandwich Islands (Hawaii). At the same time, they hoped to strengthen Great Britain's claim to the Pacific Northwest by establishing farming communities in addition to the fur trading posts. Eventually, these goals were only partially met, but the company usually did manage to make some profit.

The company directors ordered the plowing up of new cropland at "Cowlitz farm" near present-day Toledo, where an initial 1000 acres were broken and managed by Simon Plamondon. They also absorbed Fort Nisqually, where a noteworthy livestock operation was directed by Dr. William Fraser Tolmie for many years. Less important facilities were maintained elsewhere. The company's holdings were managed along the lines of a typical British colonial plantation, with a central village of laborers supervised by an overseer. The British fur traders did not encourage the development of small, independent family farms.

In 1846, with the establishment of the international boundary at the 49th parallel, the Puget's Sound Agricultural Company suddenly found its farms standing on American soil. Arrangements were made, however, to allow the British firm to continue operating in the U. S. sector for a few years, but gradually most of its holdings were parcelled out to the English, French Canadians, and French Indian crossbreeds who had been working the land.

The relocated granary in Tacoma's Point Defiance Park is a remnant from the company's Fort Nisqually operations. In fact, it may well be the only significant agricultural structure to have survived from the HBC era. North of Toledo at the site of the old "Cowlitz farm," the open prairie land remains in agricultural use today, but the historic structures are gone and the property now is divided into private ownership.

By 1837, missionaries likewise tilled the soil. Marcus Whitman, the first of a number of farmer/ missionaries, raised irrigated crops at the ill-fated Waiilatpu mission, and helped prove that agriculture was

LaFramboise Property
Antoine LaFramboise came to the Yakima Valley in 1897 as a blacksmith for a Moxee land and irrigation company. At the end of his contract he purchased property near Moxee City that included a Presbyterian church (built in 1885) which he converted into a blacksmith shop. The LaFramboise home was completed in 1902 and served as a focal point for entertainment among the area's French Canadians. (National Register)

possible in the drier environment east of the Cascades. The Whitmans provisioned not only themselves and nearby Indian encampments, but also weary immigrants following the Oregon Trail.

A legacy of the HBC and missionary period was that some Indian groups accommodated basic farming skills into traditional semi-nomadic lifeways. Kamiakin, the famous Yakima chieftain, kept gardens near the Catholic's Ahtanum mission, while Nez Perce headman Timothy irrigated crops and an orchard at Alpowa Creek on the Snake River. The Spokanes continued cultivating the soil after the Canadians abandoned Spokane House in the mid 1820s, and other Indian groups tilled ground elsewhere.

Max Steinke Round Barn

The Max Steinke round barn, built in 1916 in Whitman County, is actually dodecagonal (twelve sided), measuring sixteen -feet on a side. The walls, nine-feet-high, are constructed of reinforced concrete, and the roof is sheathed with lumber recycled from an old barn that stood nearby. The short wooden cupola, much lighter than steel versions, provided ventilation for feed stored in the loft. (National Register)

Donation Land Law and the Homestead Act

By the mid nineteenth century, settlers, miners, soldiers, stockmen, and other American frontiersmen likewise planted crops for sustenance. The immigrants arriving in the 1840s, however, had to be content for the time being with "squatting" on their new farmsteads, since there was no means whereby titles could be processed for transferring parcels of public land into private ownership. No land offices had been established, and government surveyors had yet to mark out a township and range grid system for the territory.

In 1850, the U. S. Congress began providing for these services with the passage of the Donation Land Law. This legislation granted to adult males (either native born or naturalized U. S. citizens) who had settled in the Pacific Northwest before December 1, 1846, claims of 320 acres (640 acres if married). Later immigrants received a somewhat less generous amount of 160 acres (or 320 acres if a married couple). The law only applied to the Pacific Northwest and expired in 1855, after which time (until passage of the Homestead Act in 1862) the rules were amended so that the most recent settlers had to pay $1.25 per acre to gain title after two years occupancy on a claim.

Hundreds of claims were granted under the provisions of the Donation

Land Law to settlers located west of the Cascades, since that was where population was concentrated in the 1850s. On the other hand, only a handful of Donation claims were staked out in the Columbia Plateau, mainly by former Hudson's Bay Company employees occupying scattered farmsteads in the Walla Walla, Spokane, and Colville Valleys.

In 1862, the U. S. Congress passed the Homestead Act, which proved to be the most important land legislation in the history of the West. It was under the provisions of this law that most of Washington was settled in the late nineteenth and early twentieth centuries. The Homestead Act granted up to 160 acres to any American citizen, native born or naturalized, who completed five years residency and made the required "improvements" on a claim. The only cash required in the transaction were minimal filing fees. A settler, however, could opt to "pre-empt" a claim and gain title to the land sooner, usually after only six months occupancy and by paying $1.25 per acre.

In 1873, the U. S. Congress also approved the Timber Culture Act, allowing homesteaders to claim an additional 160 acres of treeless land by planting one-fourth of it in trees within four years. Settlers residing east of the Cascades commonly took advantage of the provisions of this act.

Pioneer families constructed simple wood cabins and barns on their claims, and cleared land for crops and orchards. In the territorial era, wheat, oats, barley, hops, potatoes, dairy products, various fruits, and other basic provisions were raised on the farm and sold at military posts, lumber camps, mining towns, and other fledgling communities, or exported overseas in modest quantities from Washington's small coastal ports. Pioneer homes often served double functions as post offices, courtrooms, schools, and community meeting houses, and some homestead claims at crossroads or other key geographic locations became the sites for towns and eventually cities.

An example of a little altered agricultural frontier landscape dating from the territorial era is the Ebey's Landing National Historical Reserve, which is one of only two national historical reserves in the United States. Citizen groups and government agencies have been at work since the 1970s to protect the farms, woodlands, and vistas of this unique historic locality, where the original settler, Isaac Ebey, filed a Donation claim in 1850.

A wide range of commercial agricultural products eventually were raised on farmsteads both east and west of the Cascades. Horticulture and dairying remained important, but, in the long run, grain crops proved to be

Ebey's Landing

Colonel Isaac Ebey, one of the earliest white settlers on central Whidbey Island, served as district attorney, customs collector at Port Townsend, and captain in the state militia. In 1850, he staked out 640 acres near Coupeville, one of twenty-nine such claims filed in the area under the Donation Land Law. Today this general locality, known as Ebey's Landing, is designated a National Historical Reserve. As such, it is an outstanding example of a cultural landscape where historic buildings are preserved in near original condition and traditional farming practices are encouraged. This is one of only two national historical reserves in the United States. (National Register)

most significant. Before the century was out, the main focus of Northwest wheat farming shifted east of the Cascades, particularly to the rolling Palouse grasslands of the eastern Plateau.

By then, the open range livestock industry had suffered a series of devastating blows during the harsh winters of the 1880s, after which time the region's main agricultural activity shifted overwhelmingly to grain production. Though the prairies were largely fenced off by the end of the century, stock raising did continue to be important in some parts of central and eastern Washington. Dating from 1883, the Seivers brothers ranch near Lind is representative of a sprawling ranch complex in this era. With its array of barns, pens, sheds, bunkhouses, and other structures, the Seivers ranch was a self-sufficient community.

Perhaps no other property portrays the romance of the open range period better than the strap iron corral, a remote landmark standing on the channeled scabland prairie near Washtucna. "Uncle Jim" Kennedy, the builder of the corral, salvaged the strap iron from the dismantled Columbia and Walla Walla Railroad, which operated between Walla Walla and Wallula beginning in the early 1870s. The strap iron originally covered the tops of wooden rails on which the small engine and cars of the primitive railroad ran.

The Eastern Washington Grain Empire

The completion of the first transcontinental rail lines to the Pacific Northwest in the 1880s set the stage for eastern Washington's great agricultural boom. Washington's remarkable economic and population expansion in this era, in addition to the opening up of distant markets to its farmers, were fundamental elements in this phenomenal growth. Furthermore, the reduced freight rates of hauling by railroad allowed farmers to acquire the latest and largest farm machines then being produced by a highly competitive and innovative farm implement industry.

The transcontinental giants, particularly the Northern Pacific, held large tracts of unbroken farmland to sell to newcomers, and also sponsored town and community development projects. Their advertising agents in Europe, Canada, and the eastern United States vigorously publicized the Pacific Northwest as a land of unlimited opportunity and wealth. Soon, large numbers of American and European settlers were disembarking from immigrant trains in cities, towns, and rural crossroads all across the Columbia Plateau to stake claims.

Woolrey-Koehler Hop Kiln

From 1865 to 1891, hops were the primary commercial crop of the Puyallup Valley, providing annual harvests of 3000 pounds per acre. The Woolrey- Koehler hop kiln, constructed in 1869 of charred cedar logs, dried the crop. Wood stoves heated the entire building, including the upper level drying room and the central bailing room. In 1890, the structure was expanded and a shorter chimney added. In 1902, Carl Koehler purchased the farm and later used the kiln for bulb storage. (National Register)

Interior Grain Tramway

As dryland wheat farming flourished throughout the rolling hills and high prairies of the Palouse, ingenious methods were devised for transporting grain from the fields on the high plateau down to steamboat landings or railroad sidings along the Snake River. Built in 1901 by Aaron Kuhn, a Colfax grain merchant, this tram hauled wheat one-mile down the steep canyon walls. It operated like a modern ski lift: grain sacks loaded on "carrier" arms moved downhill on a long cable suspended from towers. Used until 1938, only weathered remnants exist today. (National Register)

Sawyer House

Elmwood Farm, built by Toppenish orchardist W. P. Sawyer in 1910, is an outstanding example of Colonial Revival architecture. The home, noteworthy for its size and setting, had an office, theater, chapel, library, parlor, living room, and six bedrooms. Window treatments were especially ornate, with leaded glass over fixed single panes on the first floor, and multi-paned double-hung windows on the second floor. The large porches with Tuscan columns provided expansive views of the property. (National Register)

The development of dryland wheat farming fortuitously coincided with the coming of the railroads. Walla Walla and Palouse area farmers had discovered that they could sow grain on the dry, and heretofore neglected, hills and high prairies. Up to the mid 1860s, farming had been restricted to the moist bottomlands, since it was erroneously believed that the endless, rolling hills were nonarable. Dryland farming entailed deep initial plowing, followed by frequent cultivation to retard moisture loss through capillary action. The adoption of this farming technique resulted in a phenomenal expansion of the wheat industry.

The Palouse hills and the Snake River country were densely settled by the early twentieth century and the large number of substantial, well-built barns, houses, and outbuildings reflected the great prosperity in these localities. Huge, cavernous barns stabled the large teams of horses and mules required to pull massive farm implements in the fields, and granaries stored harvested grain or livestock feed. Other structures included storage sheds, corrals, windmills, water tanks, and bunkhouses for hired help. An excellent example of an intact farm complex from the golden age of wheat cultivation is the well preserved Gustave Heilsberg farmstead, dating from 1904 and located near Colfax in the heart of the Palouse country.

The Desert Blooms: Central Washington Irrigation

Most of the early immigrants considered central Washington to be little more than a desert and best left to the cattlemen and their hardy stock. A few visionary settlers, however, saw great opportunities for irrigated agriculture in the broad, sagebrush-covered canyons. Consequently, by the 1880s a few sections of the semiarid landscape began blossoming with crops watered by small, pioneer-built, diversion canals that tapped the mountain streams flowing down out of the Cascades.

Soon, railroad propagandists and other regional proponents likewise were spreading the word about the agricultural potential of the dry, yet fertile, Columbia Basin. Meanwhile, private companies started irrigation schemes along the Yakima, Naches, Wenatchee, and other rivers and streams.

One settler who heard the call was Antoine LaFramboise, a French Canadian who came to the Yakima Valley in 1897 to work as a blacksmith for the Selah and Moxee Canal Company. LaFramboise later purchased land in the Moxee City area, and, while continuing a successful blacksmith trade, he and his brother Paul grew hops and experimented with tobacco. His farm complex included structures erected from 1885 to about 1910.

The private irrigation projects, however, frequently suffered from water rights disputes, insufficient funding, bad management, or inadequate engineering. These problems seriously hampered the effectiveness of many systems and caused others to fail. Consequently, the first years of the twentieth century saw increasing federal involvement in the financing, designing, and construction of large-scale irrigation projects. The U. S. Bureau of Reclamation, in particular, played a key role in the development of irrigation systems in the Yakima and Okanogan valleys. Dams were con-structed in the eastern Cascade Range, forming the Kachess, Rimrock, and other large reservoirs for water storage. The water was released as needed down-stream to the agricultural lowlands, where a complex network of canals, flumes, ditches, and electrical pumps dispersed it to the fields and orchards.

The success of irrigation systems brought prosperity to Yakima, Wenatchee, and other towns, where harvested vegetables and fruits were preserved in cold storage facilities. Standing alongside a railroad right-of-way, "fruit house row" became the hub of the produce business. Many of these historic warehouses and offices still survive, including the 1924 Holtzinger Fruit Company building in Yakima. Inside, fruit was stored, dried, or canned before shipment by rail to market.

Many homes and commercial build-ings built in this era reflected the region's growing prosperity. One of the most noteworthy was the W. P. Sawyer mansion, an impressive Colonial Revival house designed by Yakima architect W. W. DeVeaux. Constructed near Toppenish in 1910, the two-story home recalls Sawyer's New England roots with its distinguished, classically inspired details, a widow's walk, and spacious porches. Rivaling the best residences built during the same era in Seattle or Spokane, the mansion over-looked the irrigated fields of Parker

Bottom, where the enterprising Sawyer earned a fortune growing his noted Bartlett pears and other produce.

To Market: Truck Farming and Dairies

Cities grew rapidly in the late nineteenth and early twentieth centuries, providing a lucrative market for family farmers tending small-scale, but intensively cultivated, plots in the suburbs and nearby rural areas. On a regular basis, wagons (and later trucks, hence the term "truck farms" or "truck gardens") were loaded with fruits, vegetables, dairy products, and other perishable produce right off the farm. As freshness was important, the foodstuff was rushed to towns and cities to sell in local markets.

Standing on these small farmsteads were sheds for vehicles and farm tools, water storage tanks, root cellars, and greenhouses for specialized vegetable growing or floriculture. Adjoining the farm complex was the house, normally of a simple, vernacular design. Although architecturally unassuming, the family home usually was durable and spacious enough to accommodate a large and busy extended family.

Truck farming appealed to both American and immigrant farmers, but the Italians and Japanese in particular achieved prominence in the business.

Pasquale Saturno, for instance, came to the Walla Walla area in 1876 and purchased property near College Place. In time, Saturno's lucrative truck gardening operation employed not only his family, but also newly arrived Italian immigrants, giving them a start in their adopted country.

In western Washington, Japanese farmers acquired acreage in the fertile bottomlands of the Puget Sound country and supplied a large share of the fruits and vegetables sold at marketplaces in Seattle and Tacoma. These family owned agricultural operations ended during World War II, however, when all Japanese Americans on the west coast were interned.

Dairies likewise served urban wholesalers and consumers, bringing fresh milk, butter, and cheese to cities and towns for immediate sale or shipment to distant markets. Specialized structures were required on dairy farms, particularly large barns with milking stalls, mangers, grain bins, and feed rooms. Hay and cattle feed were stored in the voluminous lofts under the high gambrel, round, or arched roofs that graced these utilitarian structures.

In the twentieth century, dairying became ever more complex and mechanized, leading to the decline of many family owned operations and the rise of the corporate dairy business. The

Pacific Coast Condensed Milk Company, forerunner of the Carnation corporation, typified the new growth in the industry. Independent dairy farmers in south King County's Kent Valley brought their milk to the company's plant, where its elaborate facilities processed a variety of milk products for wide distribution throughout the region. From this beginning, Carnation continued to expand its production facilities, including development in 1910 of an experimental cattle breeding and dairy farm in the Snoqualmie Valley near the small community that still bears the company's name.

Modern supermarkets, of course, have replaced the once popular farmers' markets. An especially noteworthy exception is the Pike Place Market in Seattle. This collection of historic market stalls dates from 1907, when farmers decided to sell directly to the public along Pike Place sidewalks. Popular with consumers, the market rapidly expanded and acquired permanent facilities.

During the heyday of urban renewal schemes in the 1960s and early 1970s, national attention was focused on the city when Seattleites turned down proposals to demolish the old marketplace for a modern development project. Today, Pike Place bustles with people from all walks of life, much

as it did in the past. Shoppers still come to admire the aromas and texture of the foodstuffs, to look over merchandise, to enjoy the commotion of the crowd . . . and to go home with a few bargains.

Saturno-Breen Truck Farm

Pasquale Saturno, an Italian immigrant, arrived in College Place in 1876. He quickly purchased land and began growing vegetables (especially asparagus) and wine grapes. As his farm prospered and grew, he provided employment for other Italian immigrants. The farm still contains eight buildings dating from around 1892, including a water tower that stores 5000 gallons for household use. (National Register)

NORTH HEAD, WASH., LIGHT

Engineer Office, 13ᵗʰ L-H District
Portland, Oregon, March 24, 1896.
Tracings sent to Light-House Board with letter
of this date.

W. L. Fisk.

Capt. Corps of Engineers, U.S.A.
Engineer, 13ᵗʰ L-H District.

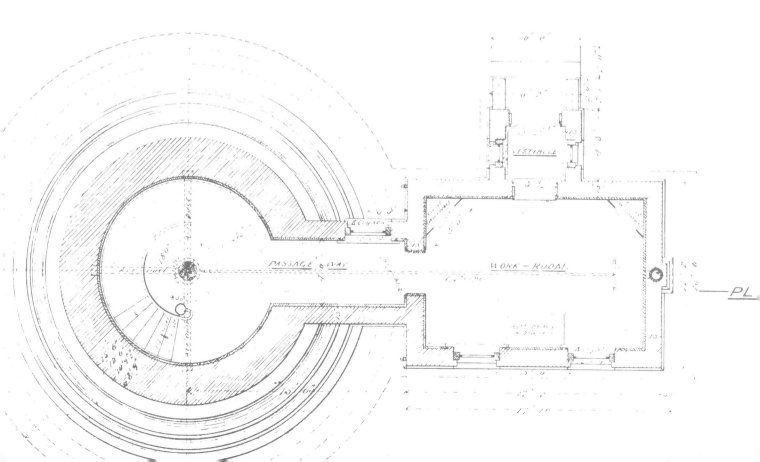

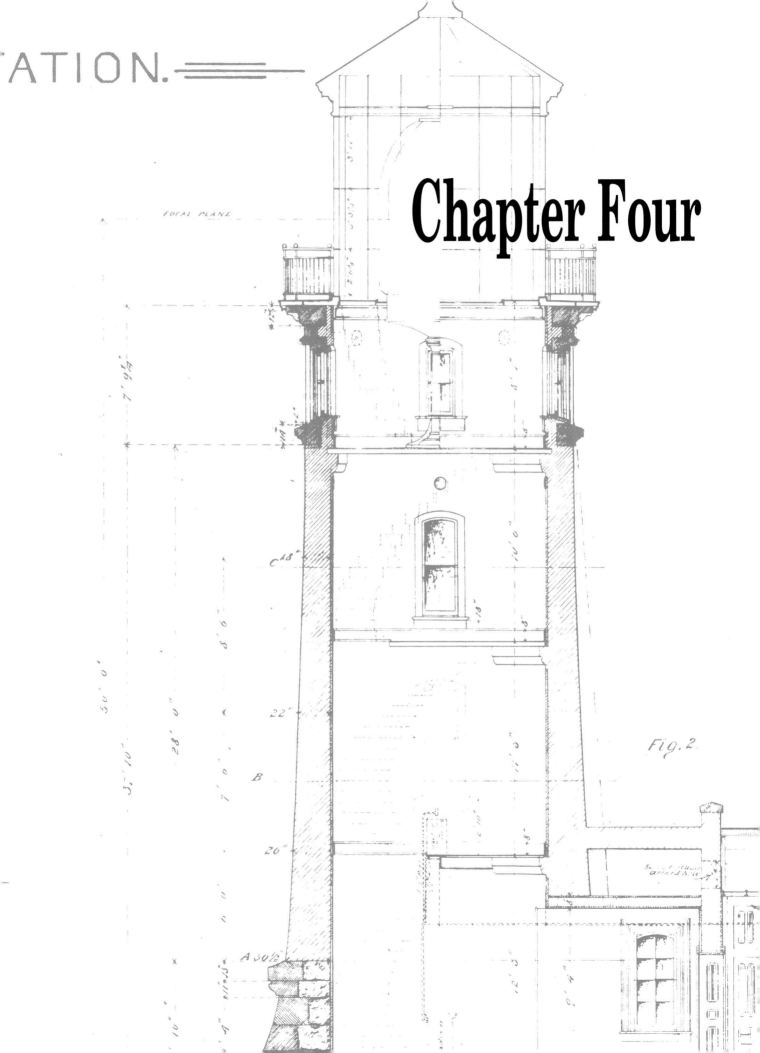

ATION.

FOCAL PLANE

Chapter Four

Fig. 2

As population expanded along Puget Sound, small vessels, or ferryboats, became a major means of transportation. More than just working vessels, these little steamers also served social and recreational needs, transporting city dwellers to beach cabins and resorts and delivering supplies and mail to rural residents. Each summer boats from the "mosquito fleet" challenged each other to races on the sound, providing off-shore entertainment for thousands of viewers crowding the beaches, piers, and boat ramps to share picnic lunches and wager on favorite vessels.

Trails, Ships, and Rails

The first settlers west of the Cascades quickly learned that travel by canoe or boat on the rivers and waterways offered the fastest and most agreeable means of getting around. In particular, the Willamette, Cowlitz, and Columbia rivers, and Puget Sound, were utilized by early pioneer watermen. Trails and roads, on the other hand, were extremely primitive or, in some localities, non-existent. On the Columbia Plateau, frontiersmen had well established, but rugged, Indian trails to follow. However, they also launched watercraft on the Snake, Pend Oreille, and Columbia rivers as well.

Corduroy Road
This corduroy road section, discovered at an archaeological excavation in Pierce County, demonstrates a frontier construction method used by a local resident. To permit easier travel in low marshy areas, the road builders felled and split trees, laying the split logs flat side down at right angles to the axis of the road. These logs were later covered with gravel or dirt to make travel more comfortable. (State Inventory)

For settlers journeying to distant Oregon City, Salem, or even Vancouver (then the political and economic centers of Oregon Territory), great difficulties were encountered en route. The road and trail systems interconnecting with the waterways were barely adequate under the best of circumstances, and practically impassable during inclement weather. In fact, this proved to be one of the reasons why settlers north of the Columbia River felt compelled to petition the U. S. Congress to carve out a separate territory. In 1853, Congress responded by creating Washington Territory out of Oregon Territory.

Washington's first territorial governor, Isaac Stevens, was well aware of the fact that improved roads and other transportation facilities were essential for sustained economic and social growth in the Pacific Northwest. In 1853, when traveling westward from the Mississippi River to take his post in Olympia, Stevens led a party of government surveyors, naturalists, artists, and soldiers in a scientific investigation of the northern Plains, Rockies, and the Pacific Northwest. The explorers surveyed routes for future wagon roads and railways, in addition to studying the flora, fauna, geology, ethnology, and climate of these regions.

The territorial legislature backed Stevens's road promotion efforts, passing measures to this end during the first and subsequent legislative sessions. Although the U. S. Congress favored new road construction in the Northwest, it fell far short in providing adequate funds. As a result, only a portion of the proposed territorial road system was completed in the early years.

Roads constructed either by private initiative or with meager public works appropriations usually were scarcely deserving of the name. In western Washington, blazing trails proved difficult in the tall, dense forest, and cutting the huge trees along a new route was laborious and dangerous. Whenever possible, trails were routed to take advantage of natural openings and level ground. Corduroy and puncheon roads, consisting of small logs laid side by side, crossed boggy areas and swamps. Grade improvements were rare, as were bridges across streams. After roads were cut through the forests, constant maintenance was required because of fallen trees, washouts, and new forest growth.

The bone jarring discomfort and other associated difficulties of traveling on these rugged and rutted, muddy or dusty, and sometimes impassable roads are well documented in the early journals and diaries. But frontier

travelers had little choice but to endure these annoyances for lack of an alternative. It was not until near the end of the territorial period that increased population and an improved economy finally allowed for the construction of adequate roads.

The Willamette and Cowlitz rivers, between the Willamette Valley and Puget Sound, developed as a primary transportation corridor at an early date. In this area, pioneers utilized both boats and wagon trails. By 1854, stagecoach and freight services were available northward from the lower Cowlitz River Valley, across the largely open prairie country of the Chehalis

Devil's Walkway
The "Goat Trail" at Devil's Corner was the most difficult stretch of a mining road that ran above the Skagit River in Whatcom County. The trail, which was blasted through a treacherous rock outcrop, led to the goldfields on the upper Skagit during the late nineteenth century, and was a spectacular example of man's determination to "tame the wilderness" and extract its riches.

watershed, and on to the fledgling outposts of civilization on southern Puget Sound. On a three day journey costing $30.00, paying passengers traveled from Portland down the Willamette and Columbia rivers to the mouth of the Cowlitz at Monticello (present-day Longview). From this point, passengers were ferried up the Cowlitz to river landings. From Cowlitz Landing (now Toledo), the rest of the journey overland to Olympia and points north was by coach, wagon, or on horseback.

Some of the other important regional trails in the early territorial period included: the Mullan Road, linking Fort Walla Walla, near the upriver limit of navigation on the Columbia, with Fort Benton in Montana, at the head of steamboat navigation on the Missouri River; the Colville Road, extending north from Walla Walla to the HBC's Fort Colvile and the U. S. Army's Fort Colville, as well as the nearby gold mining boomtown of Pinkney City; and the Caribou Trail, tracing northward from the Columbia up the Okanogan River to goldfields in the Fraser River country of British Columbia.

The main route of Northwest immigration, the Oregon Trail, which extended from Missouri to the lower Columbia Valley, primarily passed south of Washington in what is now Oregon. Only a short side trek northward to the Whitman's Waiilatpu mission and the HBC's Fort Walla Walla entered present-day Washington.

More survives than might be expected of these tracks through the forest or across sagebrush plains. For example, portions of the storied Naches Pass Trail in the Cascade Range is now used by hikers or persons driving all-terrain vehicles. This route, extending over the mountains north of Mt. Rainier, was used by immigrants in 1853, the U. S. Army in 1855, and later by ranchers driving stock westward to Puget Sound. A sense of what travel was like on early western Washington trails also can be experienced at Federation Forest State Park east of Enumclaw, where another section of the Naches Trail remains.

Due to the drier climate, more rutted sections of early trails and roads have been preserved in eastern Washington. A notable example is a short remnant of the northern branch of the Oregon Trail at the Whitman Mission National Historical Site near Walla Walla. Informed visitors with a trained eye also can find other Columbia Plateau trails: such as segments of the Mullan Road in the Palouse River watershed of east central Washington; or a section of the Nez Perce Trail east of Pomeroy, up which the Lewis and Clark Expedition led a string of Indian ponies in the spring of 1806; or the Kalispel Trail in forested Stevens and Pend Oreille counties in the northeast part of the state. The Kalispel Trail connected the Pend Oreille River and Calispell Lake with the Colville Valley, located to the west. As with so many early roads, the Kalispel Trail was an ancient Indian route used by fur traders, missionaries, soldiers, miners, packers, and other early frontiersmen.

A fascinating road dating from the turn-of-the-century farmers' frontier in southeast Washington is the Yakawawa Grade in the deep, steep-walled, Snake River canyon of Whitman County. Local wheat growers on the high plateau drove grain wagons down this long, tortuous route to a steamboat landing, and later a railroad siding, on the Snake River. Large wooden turn-tables were ingeniously constructed to enable the wagons to negotiate the extremely sharp switchback turns. Teams were driven onto these rotating platforms, which then were turned nearly 180 degrees, allowing the wagon to proceed along the next section of switchback trail. Although the turn-tables have not survived, traces of the route remain visible in Yakawawa canyon.

Sailing Ships and Steamboats

Schooners, barks, and other sailing vessels once maintained a commanding presence on Puget Sound, the lower Columbia River, and off the coast.

Curtis Wharf
Melville Curtis, an early Anacortes pioneer, began construction on the Curtis wharf in 1903. The wharf and associated buildings are closely linked with the development of marine transportation in the San Juan Islands. In the early twentieth century, the buildings served as docking facilities for the inter-island steamships which connected Anacortes with neighboring Puget Sound communities. Later, ferryboats used the wharf as a terminal for automobiles and passengers destined for Victoria and Vancouver, British Columbia. (National Register)

From the time of the founding of the earliest tidewater settlements, these ships were a primary link to the outside world, hauling mail, supplies, and passengers, and exporting Northwest timber, grain, lumber, fish, and other extractive resources to the East, California, Europe, and the Orient.

In the nineteenth century, steam-powered vessels likewise were workhorses of commerce on Washington's waterways and rivers, both east and west of the Cascades. The Hudson's Bay Company's *Beaver* was the first paddle-wheeler to ply coastal waters by 1836. Steamers pro-

Grays River Covered Bridge

Covered bridges were uncommon in Washington, and a rare surviving example is the Grays River bridge in rural Wahkiakum County. It was constructed in 1905, and the cover was added in 1908. Cables and concrete reinforcement for structural support have been added since. (National Register)

liferated with the spread of settlement in the 1850s, as local shipyards began constructing large numbers of stern-wheelers and other vessels.

By the early 1860s, during the gold strikes in the northern Bitterroots and Rockies, steamboat service was established from Portland up the Columbia to the Snake River, contributing significantly to Walla Walla's early prominence as a primary supply center for the miners. At Umatilla, located at the junction of the Umatilla and Columbia rivers, and Wallula, next to the confluence of the Columbia and the Walla Walla, thousands of miners and other passengers disembarked from stern-wheelers for the overland trek eastward to the goldfields.

By the 1880s, as the farmers' frontier spread across the Palouse hills in southeast Washington, stern-wheelers hauled out the autumn grain harvest to Portland and other lower Columbia ports. There, wheat was reloaded on oceangoing vessels for shipment to distant markets. Stern-wheeler service developed later on the upper Columbia; by 1888 the *City of Ellensburgh* had steamed as far north as Brewster. Steamers eventually chugged along the broad, forest-lined Pend Oreille River as well.

West of the Cascades, of course, steamers played an important role on Puget Sound, the lower Chehalis, the Skagit, the Columbia, and other rivers and bays. By late territorial times, steam-powered boats cruising Puget Sound provided easy passage to lumber and fishing camps and fledgling communities hidden in coves and inlets. Steamers were literally the lifeline to many of these towns and landings, isolated as they were by dense forests and difficult terrain. Supplies, mail, passengers, produce, and livestock were discharged and taken on with dutiful regularity.

The docks, whether a city pier or backwater landing, bustled with activity well into the twentieth century. A typical boat landing was Curtis wharf in Anacortes, constructed at the foot of the downtown district in 1903 and expanded several times afterward. The wharf's weathered wood siding, gabled rooflines, and worn planking still evoke images of a lively and teeming waterfront town of the early statehood era. The structure also housed a creamery, ice plant, and warehouse, and was used as a ferry terminal for the Anacortes to Sidney, British Columbia, crossing until 1961.

In time, the small Puget Sound steamers shuttling between obscure landings and major cities alike became so numerous as to be referred to as the "mosquito fleet." Though primarily working vessels, these craft also served the recreational needs of thousands. City dwellers took passage on them to summer cottages, camps, and resorts. Some larger vessels boasted hand-somely appointed interiors, serving sumptuous meals in elaborate dining salons. A standard summer entertain-ment saw the pitting of the fastest of the vessels against each other in local competitions. Crowds thronged the shoreline, piers, and boat decks to see the steamers churning away over a watery course.

This extensive fleet of vessels gradually disappeared after the widespread adoption of the automobile in the early decades of the twentieth century. However, one rare survivor is the passenger steamer *Virginia V*, built in 1922 by master shipwright Matthew Anderson. The *Virginia V*, 125-feet long with a 24-feet beam, is powered by a triple expansion reciprocating steam engine providing 400 horsepower for a top speed of 14 knots. Until 1939, the *"Ginny"* delivered groceries, mail, and passengers to a cluster of small shoreside communities on the sound between Seattle and Tacoma. After several changes in ownership, the *Virginia V* was restored in the 1950s and now plies Puget Sound on excursion cruises.

Sailing vessels operated out of Washington ports well into the twentieth century, until steamships entirely supplanted them just prior to World War II. The three-masted schooner *Wawona* is one of the few tall-masted sailing ships that has been saved, thanks to the efforts of individuals and preservation organi-zations on Puget Sound. Built in California in 1897, the *Wawona* hauled lumber between west coast ports until 1914, when Robinson Fisheries of Anacortes converted the ship for cod fishing in the Bering Sea. The *Wawona* served well in this rugged role and, by 1940, set a world's record for fish caught by a single vessel.

Lighthouses and beacons were, and remain, crucial for safe navigation in Washington's treacherous coastal waters. Today, historic lighthouses dot the coastline from Cape Disappoint-ment to the San Juan Islands, standing as reminders of the never ending struggle against the sea.

Sehome Wharf

Trails, sails, and rails all played vital roles in the economic and cultural development of Washington. In western Washington, coal was present in sufficient quantities to attract the attention of outside investors. The Bellingham Bay Improvement Company constructed the Sehome wharf to transfer coal from the Sehome mine on Lake Whatcom to ships destined for San Francisco and other distant ports. At the wharf, railroad tracks extended straight out from the bluff so that the coal train did not have to negotiate an incline to the water. Coal was dumped down long, steep chutes into the ships below. In this 1892 photograph, a Bellingham Bay & Eastern Railroad train unloads at the wharf.

Yakima Valley Transportation Company

The Yakima Valley Transportation Company is one of the last operating interurban lines in the United States and the only one left in Washington. Tied directly to the agricultural development of the Yakima Valley, the interurban transported passengers and freight from outlying orchards and farms, connecting them with the main railroad lines in Yakima. The YVTC was developed in 1907 and is now supported with local funds which maintain it in operating condition. (National Register Eligible)

Schooner *Wawona*

The *Wawona*, a three-masted schooner, was built in California in 1897. She operated in the coast lumber trade till 1914, before joining the cod fish fleet in the Bering Sea. Through 1940, the *Wawona* had caught a record 6,830,400 cod fish. In 1953, the vessel was purchased by a Montana cattle rancher and his partner, film star Gary Cooper, hopeful of using her for cattle trade with Russia. Since 1964, the *Wawona* has been owned by Save Our Ships, a preservation organization. Measuring 158-feet long, with a beam of 36-feet and a draft of more than 12-feet, the ship was never converted to mechanical power. (National Register)

The United States Life Saving Service was created in 1848 to rescue survivors from ships wrecked in coastal waters. The first such facility in Washington Territory was established near Cape Disappointment in 1873 (it stood at the present location of a U.S. Coast Guard station and rescue training school). The Klipsan Beach Life Saving Station, also in Pacific County, was first manned in 1891 and remains intact today. Now listed in the National Register of Historic Places, this compound of buildings on the Long Beach Peninsula included housing for eight men and a boathouse, from which a crew was dispatched upon receiving word of a vessel in distress.

Washington Transformed: The Railroads

Short railroad lines of only a few miles in length appeared in the Pacific Northwest by the 1850s and 1860s. They aided steamboat navigation on the Columbia River by hauling freight around impassible rapids at the Cascades and The Dalles. In the early 1870s, the rustic Walla Walla and Columbia Railroad also started operations, hauling grain and merchandise on tottering railway cars between Walla Walla and a stern-wheeler landing at Wallula on the Columbia.

These diminutive rail lines played a key role in the development of the local frontier economy, but the fact remained that Washington was cut off from most supplies and manufactured goods available in the East. Sustained growth and prosperity could only be achieved when the region developed transcontinental railway connections with the rest of the United States.

This vital link finally materialized in 1883, when the Northern Pacific Railroad and the Oregon Railway and Navigation Company (OR&N) combined to complete the first northern transcontinental route. The Northern Pacific laid tracks from Minnesota, across the northern Plains and Rockies, and through Spokane to Wallula on the Columbia. From that point, OR&N rails extended through the Columbia gorge to the Portland vicinity, near where a spur line continued northward to Tacoma.

Within a few years, the Northern Pacific built another line directly over the Cascade Range, via the Yakima Valley and Stampede Pass to Puget Sound. Other transcontinental railroads likewise penetrated the region, including the Union Pacific in the early 1880s, the Great Northern in 1893, and the Milwaukee in 1909. Numerous branch lines proliferated across the state as well.

The transcontinental railroads triggered three decades of astounding economic and social expansion.

Liberty Stage Office

The town of Liberty in Kittitas County is the best remaining example of a gold mining town in Washington. The stage and livery stable office was constructed in the mid 1890s. This little one-room structure, built of rough sawn lumber with a shake roof, is one of a dozen buildings included in the Liberty Historic District. (National Register)

Washington's growth rate in the 1880s was greater than in any other section of the nation. The state's population of 75,116 in 1880 expanded to 1,141,990 by 1910, a fifteen-fold increase. Railroads brought in tens of thousands of home-seekers, stimulated tremendous urban and rural growth, and quickened the development of the region's great agricultural and timber resources.

Seattle, Spokane, and Tacoma emerged as dominant population and commercial centers. Their elaborate railway stations rivalled any in the nation for architectural scaling and decorative details. Today, the Union Depot-Warehouse Historic District in Tacoma is probably Washington's best surviving example of the intense commercial development spurred by a train station and rail yards.

Scores of towns blossomed and prospered around the new railroad depots. The Old North Yakima Historic District in Yakima illustrates how a train station served as the focus for a community's social and economic life. Directly across from the large, attractive depot stood hotels, restaurants, theaters, and mercantile establishments, which thrived on the bustle generated by rail traffic. Immediately to the west sprawled rows of busy fruit warehouses, from which agricultural produce was shipped to regional and national markets.

Urban rail transit systems also were developed in the late nineteenth century as cities grew ever larger. By the 1890s, electric-powered trolleys replaced the horse-drawn railcars originally used on these public transit lines. Close on the heels of urban streetcar development came the interurban lines. These electrically-powered systems were essentially long-distance streetcar lines that linked urban centers with the suburbs and rural hinterlands.

Spokane served as the hub for interurban tracks extending south to Whitman County, east into Idaho, and north to an amusement park and lake resorts. A network of interurban lines likewise stretched between Tacoma and

Bellingham. The Terminal Building, in Seattle's Pioneer Square, stood at an end of a busy Puget Sound interurban route.

A handful of interurban depots, transformer stations, and associated features yet survive. One example is the Washington Water Power Company's Cheney depot, built in 1907 on the Spokane, Medical Lake, and Cheney route. Besides a waiting room and ticket office, the building contained storage space for perishables and other freight.

Railroads dominated intercity and interstate transportation well into the twentieth century. By the 1920s, however, the increased use of automobiles and trucks spelled doom for most trolleys, and signalled the beginning of a long decline for America's once mighty railroad transportation network.

Today, the Yakima Valley Transportation Company, or YVTC, is one of the last interurban lines in the nation. The electric-powered railway was conceived in 1907 by a group of bankers and real estate entrepreneurs eager to promote local development. Initially, the system's three miles of track only served passengers. After the line was taken over by the Union Pacific in 1909, an infusion of money from the corporate giant allowed for the construction of extensive substations, car barns, and repair shops, and the extension of the tracks to such suburban districts as Selah and Fruitvale, with their flourishing orchards, ranches, and sawmills. From these outlying locations, YVTC cars transported produce and lumber, as well as passengers, to the railway hub in Yakima.

By 1920, at the height of its development, the YVTC extended 48 miles through the Yakima Valley, contributing significantly to the growth and development of the area's agricultural and industrial economy. Though interurban passenger service was discontinued in 1935, the YVTC hauled freight until 1983. In recent years, concerned Yakima citizens have championed the line's preservation and sponsor trolley excursions on summer weekends.

Modern Transportation: Automobiles and Airplanes

By the 1910s, the mass production of cars by Ford and other large automobile manufacturers led to an ever increasing number of vehicles on Washington roadways. Early motorists, however, were frustrated with the narrow, crooked, unimproved roads remaining from the horse and buggy days of the nineteenth century. In fact, automobile owners voiced some of the same complaints about roads as the early settlers did about trails in the 1850s. By the 1910s, highway construction and bridge building projects rapidly increased.

Brick and macadam were utilized in paving the first roadways for motorized traffic. Most of these original surfaces, of course, now are covered over with modern paving materials, but a remnant of an early twentieth-century red brick highway has been restored on 196th Avenue SE in King County. Originally known as the Yellowstone Road, it serves residents of a suburban neighborhood near Redmond. Constructed in 1913, this section of road was part of the national Yellowstone Trail, which at that time was the northernmost of four new transcontinental roadways extending across the country. The route stretched 3300 miles from Boston to Seattle.

In the 1930s, great progress continued to be made in road construction as federal, state, and local agencies sponsored numerous bridge and highway projects, providing employment for thousands of workers during the Great Depression.

Also in this era, air travel played an increasingly important role in the state's commerce, as did aircraft production in the region's industrial growth. By the early 1940s, the Boeing Airplane Company, based in Seattle, became one of the state's leading employers. Today, Boeing transport planes dominate the national and international aircraft travel industry.

William E. Boeing, an independently wealthy young man who early on became fascinated with flying, built his first airplane in 1916 as head of the Pacific Aero Products Company. In 1917, the name was changed to the Boeing Airplane Company. After World War I, Boeing landed lucrative government airmail contracts to cities in the West. Gradually, orders for military and passenger craft earned for the Boeing company a reputation for dependability and quality. Boeing's dominant position in the aviation industry was solidified during World War II, when the B-17 "Flying Fortress" and the B-29 "Super Fortress" bombers performed admirably in Europe and the Pacific.

The "Red Barn" at Seattle's Boeing Field is closely tied to the history of William Boeing and early aviation in the Pacific Northwest. Originally constructed in 1909 as a boathouse for the E. W. Heath shipyard on the Duwamish River, the building was acquired by Boeing in 1910 and used for completing his yacht. In 1915, Boeing converted the structure into an office and assembly facility for the fabrication of his first aircraft. This structure, which played a seminal role in aviation history, today is preserved as part of Seattle's Museum of Flight complex.

Washington witnessed other milestones in aviation history as well. A monument at Vancouver's Pearson Field, for example, commemorates the Chkalov transpolar flight from Moscow, which landed at the city's airport next to the Columbia River on June 20, 1937. Though certain episodes about the flight across the North Pole are shrouded in mystery, the Vancouver memorial is a rare American monument honoring a Soviet achievement.

Some years earlier, in 1924, the Sand Point Naval Air Station in Seattle was the takeoff point and terminus of a round-the-world flight by U. S. military aviators. Four airmen and two aircraft completed the 27,534 mile journey, which included a 585 mile nonstop segment over the Pacific Ocean. The trans-world flight was notable not only for setting a distance record, but also for the cooperation demonstrated by the many nations assisting the pilots in their pioneering effort.

Union Station
One of the state's best known architectural landmarks, Tacoma's copper-domed Union Station was designed by noted architects Charles Reed and Alan Stem of St. Paul. Construction began in 1910, and it was completed in 1911. The station was the western terminus of the Northern Pacific Railroad, and it currently is being restored with federal, state, and local governmental support. (National Register)

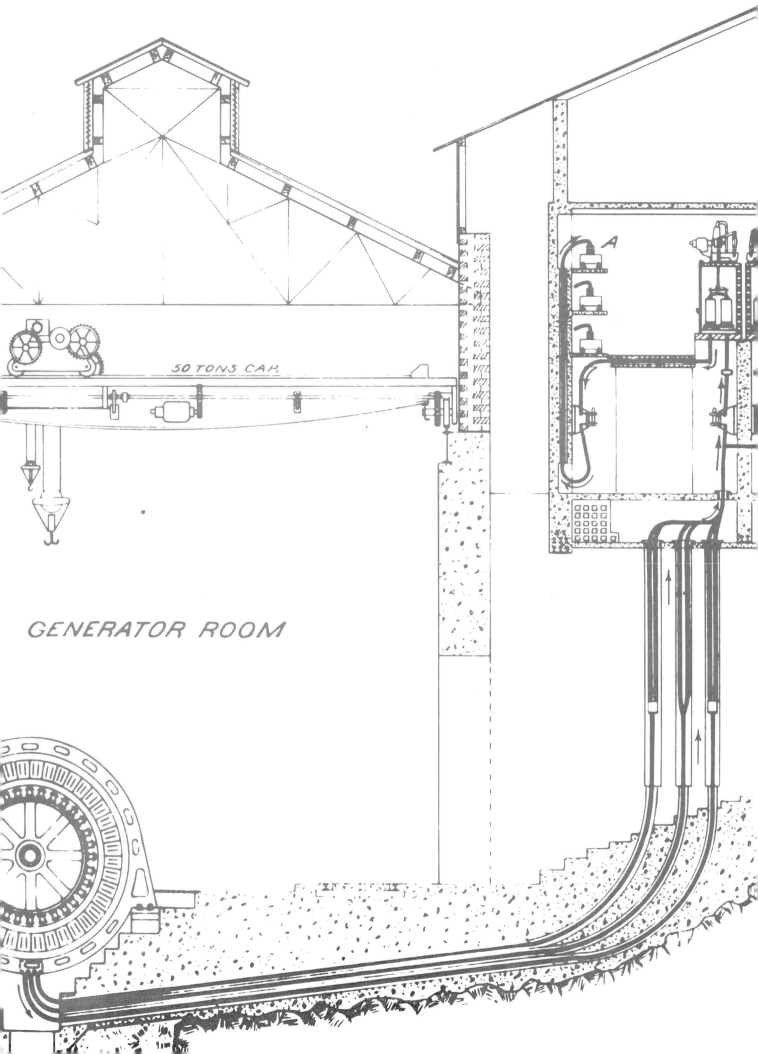

50 TONS CAP.

GENERATOR ROOM

A

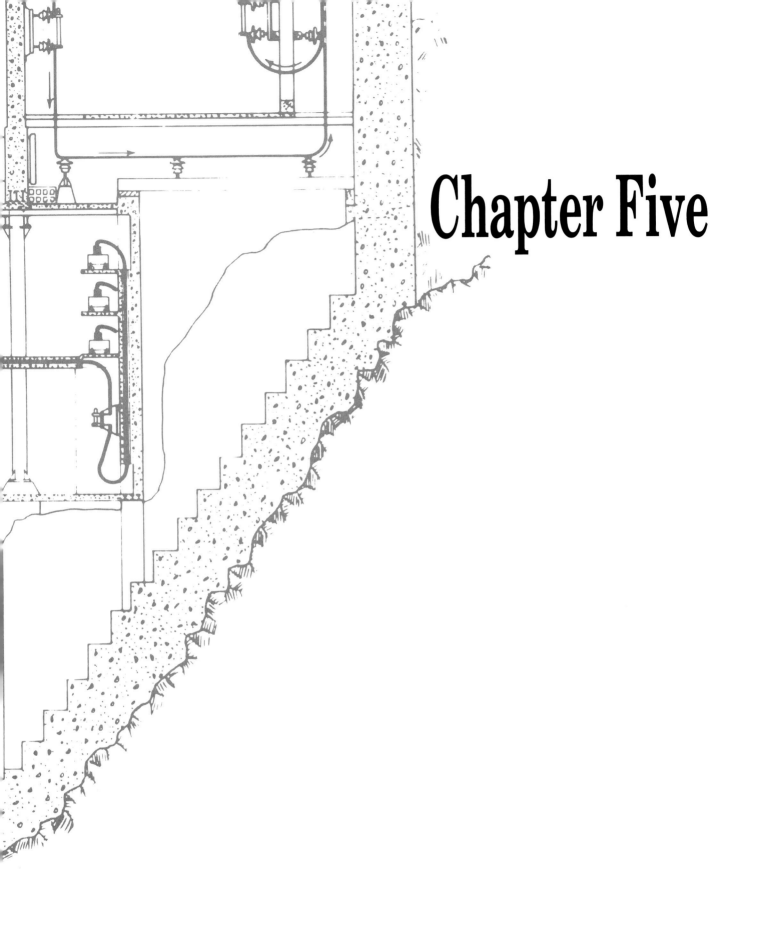

Chapter Five

Dickman Headsaw

This headsaw from the Dickman Company sawmill in Tacoma cut up to 150,000 board feet of lumber a day. Between 1923 and 1977, it cut enough lumber to build all the housing in a city the size of Tacoma. Standing 34-feet high, with a 15-inch blade and wheels 10-feet in diameter, this "first cut" saw was indispensable in handling the Pacific Northwest's large trees. It took five men to change and sharpen the blade. Twice daily they removed a blade, rolled a newly sharpened one from the filing room to the huge saw, and slipped it over the wheel. (National Register)

Factories, Mines, and Mills

Early settlers west of the Cascades recognized the potential wealth in the great forests bordering the rivers and saltwater passages and extending back into the high mountain ranges. The first loggers worked along the shorelines, dropping trees directly into rivers and bays. During the California gold rush, small sailing ships carried cargoes of timber to San Francisco from the still nameless collection of cabins that became Seattle and from other tidewater lumbering operations as well. Long, straight spars cut in coastal areas also were in demand for use as masts in American and European shipyards.

Steam-powered sawmills multiplied after the 1860s, as the demand for lumber grew, and, by the 1880s, timber companies and independent loggers alike were cutting trees from the Columbia River to the Canadian border. In the early days on Puget Sound alone, a fleet of almost 150 vessels carried lumber to all parts of the world. The coming of the transcontinental railroads in the late nineteenth century, the decline of lumbering in the East and the Great Lakes regions, and the opening of the Panama Canal in 1915 all stimulated the growth of markets for Pacific Northwest wood products.

In the nineteenth century, logs were dragged out of the woods on log-lined "skid roads" by oxen, horses, and mules, or floated down streams to waiting sawmills. Centuries-old Douglas fir, spruce, and cedar were cut, but hemlock, because it was a soft, light, splintery wood, was considered waste and good only for camp construction and skid roads. The pioneer loggers could not foresee that hemlock would one day become a mainstay of the lumber industry.

Early logging outfits were directed by the "boss," usually an old hand from Michigan or Maine who knew how to handle the tough, spirited, but hard-working, "fallers" who with axe and saw dropped the trees, the "buckers" who cut them into manageable lengths, and the "bull whackers" who led the teams that pulled the logs out of the forest.

Skid road builders followed near the fallers, laying down hemlock logs in the earth at spaced intervals where needed. Young men called "grease monkeys," with bucket and brush in hand, kept the skid roads well oiled, while other workers mortised in pieces of maple as the skids broke or wore out. Only straight and smooth logs could be dragged on the skid roads by the bull whackers and their teams; thus, the fallers, while standing on springboards placed in notches in the bark, cut trees well above the spreading stump, a wasteful, but necessary, practice.

Removing trees from the steeper, less accessible terrain was impractical because of the slow hauling techniques and prohibitive costs. With the introduction of narrow-gauge logging railroads at about the turn of the century, however, even remote timber stands in rugged localities were opened up to the lumbermen.

Small locomotives pulling long lines of log cars soon proliferated throughout the forests of eastern and western Washington. Thousands of short railway spurs spread out from the camps and sawmills into any canyon or valley, or onto any plateau and ridge, where trees could be cut and skidded to sidings. Railway grades, trestles, and bridges constantly were being built mile by mile into the virgin forests, and just as quickly torn up or abandoned after the loggers cut the timber.

Tall-stacked steam donkey engines, standing on skids, allowed the introduction of high-lead (or high-line) logging, which supplanted the difficult and wasteful ground-lead system. In high-lead yarding, capstans on steam donkeys pulled cables through tackle on spar trees, moving logs along well above the ground to railroad loading sites and thus preventing "hang ups" with debris and obstacles on the forest floor.

Steam donkeys, company owned railroads, and high-lead logging prevailed during the heyday of the Pacific Northwest timber industry in the first four decades of the twentieth century. Interestingly enough, fallers continued to cut down trees by hand with axe and saw. It was not until the early 1940s that gasoline-powered chain saws became light and efficient enough to be used in the woods. In addition, manpower shortages during World War II encouraged the adoption of chain saws in the undermanned lumber industry.

After the logs were hauled out of the woods, they were stored in piles in yarding areas or dropped in ponds at the sawmills. When the logs were

maneuvered into the sawmill itself, headsaws, gang saws, and other elaborate machinery cut them into everything from barrel staves to bridge timbers.

Logging had become much more efficient in the early twentieth century, but the use of railroads and steam engines also greatly increased the fire danger. Government and private fire protection agencies alleviated the situation somewhat, but it was not until diesel- and gasoline-powered trucks and tractors became prevalent just prior to World War II that the fire danger was significantly reduced. Trucks and tractors emitted far fewer sparks, and the many new roads and highways aided fire crews in arriving quickly at the site of a burn.

F. Arnold
Polson House
Constructed in 1923 with lumber from the family's own mills, this home was a wedding gift from an uncle to Polson and his wife. Four fireplaces faced with Italian tiles heated the house, and the floorboards are thirty-feet long hemlock strips. (National Register)

Tenino Stone Quarry
Of the more than 250 commercial stone quarries operating in the state during the last century, few lasted more than several years. The Tenino Stone Company quarry was active from 1888 to 1926, and owed its longevity to the proximity of a rail line, as well as the superior quality of its stone. Throughout the Northwest, many buildings still stand which were crafted from Tenino sandstone. Today the quarry site is used as a municipal swimming pool. (National Register)

Today, giant stumps and faint traces of railway grades still remain in the dark forests as monuments to the boom days of logging. Generally, the environmental conditions of the Northwest woods, as well as the transitory nature of the timber industry itself, have not been conducive to the preservation of features associated with logging history. The skid roads and railroad grades were quickly overgrown by second growth after they were abandoned. Logging camps were mobile and hauled off to other localities after the trees were cut. Fire destroyed innumerable sawmills. Sometimes mills were rebuilt, but frequently the ruins simply were abandoned if the local supply of trees had dwindled. Today, an old sawmill site often is a chaotic jumble of concrete foundations, twisted machinery, and metal, all thickly overgrown and badly weathered.

Some excellent remnants of lumbering history still exist, of course, such as the Dickman Company head-saw, now preserved in Tacoma. Saws of this type took the first cuts out of big logs. Weighing fifteen tons and standing about thirty-four-feet high, the Dickman saw was produced by the Sumner Iron Works of Everett and installed in 1923. When the mill burned in 1979, the undamaged headsaw was removed and relocated in a park, where it remains today on public display.

Many reminders of the historic role of lumbering in the Pacific Northwest actually can be found in urban areas, since whole communities grew up around, or were supported by, sawmilling and lumbering activities. Port Gamble, a lumber town located near the tip of the Kitsap Peninsula, was established by timbermen from the East, and today it retains a distinctive New England flavor. Camp Grisdale, standing in the foothills of the Olympic Mountains, operated until the 1980s as the last of the company owned logging communities. Many mill towns, of course, now are completely gone; for example, no visible trace remains of the once busy lumber port of Port Blakely on Bainbridge Island. Others, like Upper Fairfax in Pierce County and Selleck in King County, retain only a few houses or other structures located near an abandoned mill site.

Larger cities, such as Seattle, Everett, Spokane, and Tacoma, owed much of their financial success to the forests, as did smaller communities situated on Grays Harbor, Willapa Bay, Puget Sound, and elsewhere, particularly, but not exclusively, in western Washington. Lumber companies established their headquarters buildings, offices, and other facilities in these towns (e.g., the Lumber Exchange Building in South Bend). And, it was there that mill owners, managers, and

other employees built their residences, such as the F. Arnold Polson house of Hoquiam, the Neil Cooney home (Spruce Cottage) in nearby Cosmopolis, the R. D. Merrill house of Seattle, the Salsich Lumber Company Superintendent's house in Yelm, and the Weyerhaeuser mansion (Haddaway Hall) in Tacoma. These properties reflected the great wealth that the forest industry generated for the Pacific Northwest economy.

Mining

Beginning in territorial times, there were wild-eyed expectations that the development of Washington's mineral

Roslyn Historic District
The town of Roslyn in Kittitas County thrived with the large-scale development of coal mines between 1886 and 1920. Most of the 600 or more framed residences and commercial and community structures consist of building materials produced locally. The lumber was from surrounding forests; the sandstone was acquired from outcroppings above town; and brick was manufactured at the Gunther Brick Mill in nearby Cle Elum. (National Register)

Thorp Grist Mill
The Thorp grist mill, built in 1883 in Kittitas County, may well be the oldest intact grist mill in the state. The waterpowered turbine dates from 1898, and the mill remained in use until 1944, grinding local grains into feed and flour. (National Register)

resources would play a major role in the regional economy. In fact, as recently as the first decade of the twentieth century many considered mining, and not logging, to be the main economic focus of the Cascade Range. Enough subsurface wealth was found in the mountains to lure and tantalize prospectors, mine operators, developers, and investors, but, in most cases, the veins never went deep enough to fulfill their inflated hopes. Gold, silver, copper, coal, iron—even oil—beckoned strongly at different times.

In the 1850s, gold strikes along the creeks and rivers in the Cascades and the Inland Empire attracted thousands of miners, many of them veterans of the California gold rush, to wash the placers for riches. The easy pickings were cleaned up in several years and most of the miners moved on, leaving the exhausted claims and the more difficult deposits to be worked over by Chinese miners or, in later decades, by mining engineers with huge dredges and other heavy equipment. Chinese miners frequently left evidences of their passing in the form of long, linear piles of stones and boulders alongside the streams. Using pulleys and derricks, the Chinese hauled obstructing rocks out of the riverbeds and shoreline terraces and stacked them nearby, in order to work the gold-bearing sands and dirt.

By the 1880s, quartz mining surpassed placer mining in importance, requiring large-scale investments, often including eastern capital, to develop copper, nickel, cobalt, cinnabar, and other ores. Thousands of prospectors and miners struggled into the highlands via ancient Indian and game trails, or by cutting their way through the rocky and thickly forested canyons. By the turn of the century, miners had thoroughly explored all of the state's mountainous regions, hacking out new trails and roads and developing mines, concentrating mills, and short-lived boomtowns.

As with logging remains, evidences of historic mining activities are not always easy to find on the landscape. Often, claims were worked over again with new equipment and techniques, which destroyed earlier remnants. Vegetation, fires, erosion, weathering, and avalanches have obliterated many other sites. But, as always, some features have survived.

The town of Liberty, located in the eastern foothills of the Cascade Range in Kittitas County, is a community originally devoted entirely to gold mining. First organized in 1873, the rambling collection of log cabins and simple frame buildings housed miners who worked claims over long periods of time. Nearby are the Virden and Blewett arrastras, simple devices used to crush ore-bearing rock to release the minerals. Arrastras consisted of large stone basins, in which quartz was crushed by stones dragged in a circular fashion. The pulverized ore normally was washed through sluice boxes, and the precious metal was recovered by amalgamation with mercury. Spanish and Mexican in origin, arrastras were introduced in the western mining regions at the time of the California gold rush.

In quartz mining, however, the use of more complex technological processes

Beehive Ovens
Irondale was one of several iron and steel mills built in western Washington in the late nineteenth century. From 1880 to 1910, coke was produced in the huge beehive ovens for use in smeltering. (Razed: Irondale Historic District, National Register)

normally was the rule. Ore cars shuttled back and forth over a system of light gauge railway tracks from the mine to a nearby processing plant or smelter, which frequently was contained in a large building standing on a massive stone or concrete foundation. In the concentrating mills, large batteries of stamping machines and rollers pulverized the rock. Other equipment then sorted, roasted, leached, and collected the minerals to complete the smelting process.

When no longer needed at a specific site, the stamp mills, rollers, and concentrating equipment normally were pulled out and hauled off to other locations, while the building itself was razed or abandoned. These large-scale mining operations, of course, frequently left recognizable traces on the land-

Electron Flume

As demand for hydropower increased, extensive and innovative networks of flumes and canals were constructed around the state. In 1903, this ten-mile-long wooden flume was built to divert water for a hydroelectric plant in the Puyallup watershed at Electron. The spectacular structure required constant maintenance by a crew riding in railroad cars atop its massive timbers. In some places, the trestles were eighty-feet high. In 1984-1985, much of the flume was rebuilt with metal materials. (State Inventory)

Chinese Walls

Built in Okanogan County between 1889 and 1892, the "Chinese Walls" are not associated with Chinese, nor are they simple walls. They actually are a series of foundation terraces for buildings intended to be built near Ruby for refining silver ore. Consisting of local rough-cut granite, these stone features ascend the slope in seven tiers, the tallest of which is 27- feet high and 194-feet long at the broadest extent. (State Inventory)

Snoqualmie Falls Generating Station

In its early days of operation, the Snoqualmie Falls generating station provided power to the greater Seattle and Tacoma areas, but it was the street railway systems that were the main users of the electricity produced by this plant. Generating equipment for the station is enclosed in a narrow chamber excavated in 1898 about 250-feet below the Snoqualmie River. The unique underground location was chosen to provide a completely dry atmosphere with a constant temperature. The plant remains in operation today. (National Register)

scape. A good example is the so-called "Chinese Walls" site in Okanogan County, where a complex of stone walls jut out of a hillside. They were meant to be the foundations for a silver concentrator, developed by the Arlington Mill Company in 1889, but the facility never was completed. Looking very much like the Great Wall of China, the impressive, rough-cut, granite walls are almost thirty-feet high in places and from three- to four-feet thick.

As with the lumber industry, significant buildings associated with mining history are located in towns and cities. Lead and zinc mining operations, for example, were directed from the Pend Oreille Mines building in Metaline Falls. Spokane, in particular, benefited enormously from the fabulous wealth coming out of the silver mines of northern Idaho. Most of the important mining entrepreneurs and developers resided in the city in grand and impressive residences, such as the Clark mansion and other elaborate homes in exclusive neighborhoods like Brown's Addition.

The convoluted geology of the Cascade Range and the Puget Sound lowland also held seams of coal, which miners exploited by the late nineteenth century. Communities grew up to support the mines, and today one of the best preserved is Roslyn, a picturesque mining town in the upper Yakima River watershed of the eastern Cascade foothills. Roslyn, with its wood frame houses scattered along a series of steeply pitched streets above a brick commercial center, was a company town that supplied vast amounts of coal to run Washington's spreading network of railroads. At the center of the community stands the Northwest Improvement Company store, which carried most of the goods and supplies needed by the townspeople. Roslyn was an ethnic and racial melting pot, with distinct neighborhoods and cemeteries for blacks, Italians, and other nationalities that rubbed shoulders on the streets and in the mines.

In the western Cascades, coal mining also gave rise to a number of towns. Some remain, like Black Diamond. Others are gone, such as Tono, which itself has succumbed to a modern strip mining operation near Centralia. At Newcastle only a single house now stands. Identified as Pacific Coast Company house #75, it is a rare example of the type of residence that was occupied by miners and their families in the 1870s.

Cascade coal varied greatly in quality. An excellent grade of coal was found at Roslyn, where the deposits were deep and expensive to mine. Elsewhere in Washington, less desirable grades of coal were common, which left considerable residue when

Irondale Housing
These modest cottages were constructed around 1902 to house Irondale Steel Company superintendents, and are now included in the Irondale Historic District. The works employed between 100 and 300 people and was responsible for the significant growth of the Irondale community. There is little other evidence left of this once prosperous town. (Irondale Historic District, National Register)

Peter Kirk platted a townsite on the eastern shore of Lake Washington in preparation for establishing an ironworks facility. The visionary Kirk hoped to supply steel rails to the western United States, China, and South America. The mill never was built, however, although homes and commercial buildings went up along the newly surveyed streets. Today, the Kirk Building, the Sears Building, the Masonic Lodge, and several residences date from the early years of Kirkland's founding.

The iron and steel mill at Irondale, located just south of Port Townsend, was more successful. Industrial activity began at Irondale in 1879 with the smelting of bog iron from ore deposits in the Chimacum Valley. The first blast furnace went into production two years later. The plant continued to operate sporadically until 1919, when it finally closed for good. The local sources of iron ore and coal were not of sufficient quality or quantity to produce an entirely satisfactory product, and the competition from the well-established Eastern steel industry was stiff. Despite its passing, the Irondale plant was a significant attempt to introduce heavy industry in Washington.

Today, crumbling brick and concrete foundations hidden by brush and trees are all that remain of the plant,

burned. Nevertheless, these deposits were easily developed, and the coal was widely sold on the commercial market.

Northwest coal made good coke for industrial applications, and several coking operations were started in eastern Pierce County at Wilkeson, Carbonado, and Fairfax, where long rows of beehive-shaped ovens flanked railroad tracks. Railway cars brought coal from the mines to the ovens where it was baked to drive off impurities. When the coke cooled, the same rail lines transported the coke to industrial sites on Puget Sound.

The availability of local coal and coke inspired some developers to attempt to develop an iron and steel industry in the Pacific Northwest. In 1888, for example, although company houses yet stand adjacent to the site and are occupied. The commercial district also is gone, and it now is difficult to imagine that Irondale once was a thriving town with busy docks and daily steamer traffic.

Other Extractive Industries

Brickyards, quarries, lime works, and cement plants likewise have produced basic construction materials for an ever expanding regional economy. By the turn of the century, virtually every sizeable town and city had at least one brickyard, and, in the rush of building some boomtowns, bricks sometimes were fired in the streets right at the construction sites.

More durable bricks, however, were produced at larger, more substantial plants, where the manufacturing process could be carefully monitored, and the volume of production was high. The American Firebrick Company near Spokane was typical of these larger facilities. The present plant was established in 1902 and retains five kilns dating from before 1911. The facility produced brick and other clay products not only for the Spokane market, but also for shipment to Seattle, Portland, Boise, and British Columbia.

Lime, derived from limestone, was utilized in the making of brick mortar, wall plaster, steel, cement, and glass. An especially valuable source of lime-stone is located on San Juan Island, where, during the British-American "Pig War" boundary dispute of the 1860s, English soldiers burned and calcined limestone for their own needs. Primary development of the regional lime industry began in 1886 with the formation of the Roche Harbor Lime Company. For the next half century, this company manufactured and shipped lime to widespread markets. The firm had the largest payroll in the county, and it developed Roche Harbor into a company town. Although lime is no longer produced at the site, Roche Harbor's kilns, hotel, workers cottages, and principal residences largely remain intact, even though the community now has become a first-class resort for boaters and other visitors to San Juan Island.

Before concrete was widely introduced, stone was the building material of choice for the foundations, walls, and decorative detailing of substantial structures. Although numerous rock outcrops throughout the state were utilized for local needs, there were three major quarries that provided high quality, finished stone for construction: Tenino (near Olympia), Wilkeson (in eastern Pierce County), and Chuckanut (near Bellingham). Beginning in the 1880s, men and machines at the quarries cut out slabs of fine grained stone, which then were finished as smooth dressed blocks or carved in decorative relief. Cut stone from the quarries was utilized in the construction of many of Washington's most important public and private buildings well into the twentieth century.

Steam and Electrical Power

For many years, steam engines powered the belts, shafts, and gears of the heavy machinery used in Washington's sawmills, quarries, and other industries. The big engines designed on the Corliss pattern, in par-ticular, were dramatic in appearance because of their large impressive flywheels. An excellent remaining example is on public display in downtown Newport in Pend Oreille County. Newport's Corliss engine, with its sixteen-feet diameter wheel, remained in continuous service for fifty-five years, supplying power to saws that cut one billion board feet of lumber.

Steam power was supplemented and eventually replaced by another basic source of power that could do much more, namely, electrical engines. Washington's abundant water resources, of course, allowed for the widespread development of hydro-electric power. The earliest, local hydroelectric systems were modest operations, developed mainly for providing community lighting systems, but, in time, more ambitious power projects were developed with industrial applications in mind.

The limited, less efficient efforts of the 1870s and mid 1880s quickly gave way to improved electrical facilities made possible by the introduction of alternating current. Spokane's Monroe Street Plant, completed in 1889 at a site next to mighty Spokane Falls, was one of the first large generating stations in Washington and among the first to transmit in alternating current. It since has been substantially reconstructed, and its early equipment was removed.

Another particularly impressive power generating plant, the Snoqualmie Falls cavity generating station, was put into service in 1898. Located in a huge man-made chamber cut into solid rock 250-feet below the top of the falls, it is unique not only for its design, but also because much of the original facility remains in use today.

Innovative engineering was a hallmark of Northwest hydroelectric projects. Long, extensive networks of canals, tunnels, and flumes brought water to power the turbines; the ten-mile-long wooden flume at Electron, for example, is the longest power-facility flume in the state. An original White River installation in western Washington included a seven-mile-long network of timber flumes, lined and unlined canals, and settling basins. The Long Lake Dam west of Spokane reputedly had the highest spillway

Georgetown Steam Plant
The imposing Georgetown Steam Plant was built in 1906 by the Seattle Electric Company. Designed by Stone and Webster Engineering Corporation of Boston Massachusetts, the plant's Curtis steam turbo-generators are the last operating examples of the world's first large-scale steam turbines. Used regularly during World War II and briefly for standby power up to the early 1960s, the plant is now maintained as an industrial museum. (National Register and National Historic Landmark)

(208-feet) in existence when it was completed in 1915. When the Cushman Dam on the Olympic Peninsula was completed in 1929, it was hailed as the highest concrete arch dam (280-feet) in the world. Such projects, of course, provided the foundation for the economic and social prosperity of communities in every corner of the state.

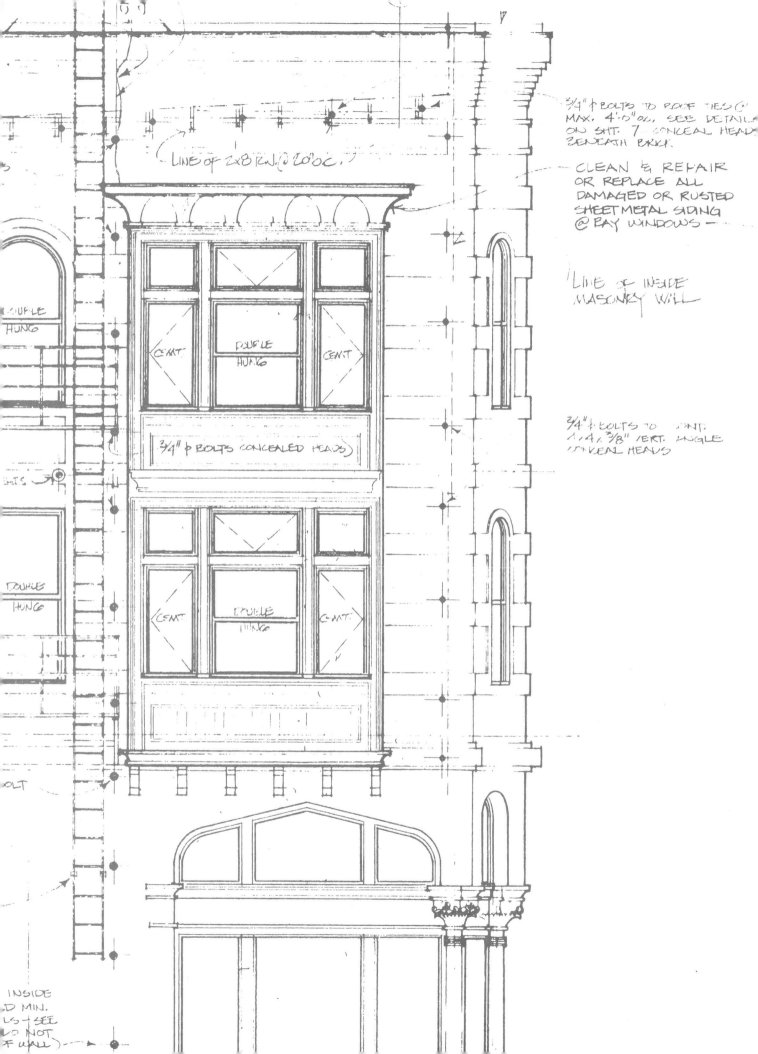

LINE OF 2x8 P.W. @ 20"OC.

3/4"ø BOLTS TO ROOF TIES @ MAX. 4'-0"OC. SEE DETAILS ON SHT. 7 CONCEAL HEADS BENEATH BRICK.

CLEAN & REPAIR OR REPLACE ALL DAMAGED OR RUSTED SHEET METAL SIDING @ BAY WINDOWS —

LINE OF INSIDE MASONRY WALL

3/4"ø BOLTS TO CONT. 4x4x3/8" VERT. ANGLE CONCEAL HEADS

DOUBLE HUNG

CEM'T

DOUBLE HUNG

CEM'T

3/4"ø BOLTS (CONCEALED HEADS)

CEM'T

DOUBLE HUNG

CEM'T

DOUBLE HUNG

DOUBLE HUNG

INSIDE D MIN. LS + SEE O NOT F WALL)

BOLT

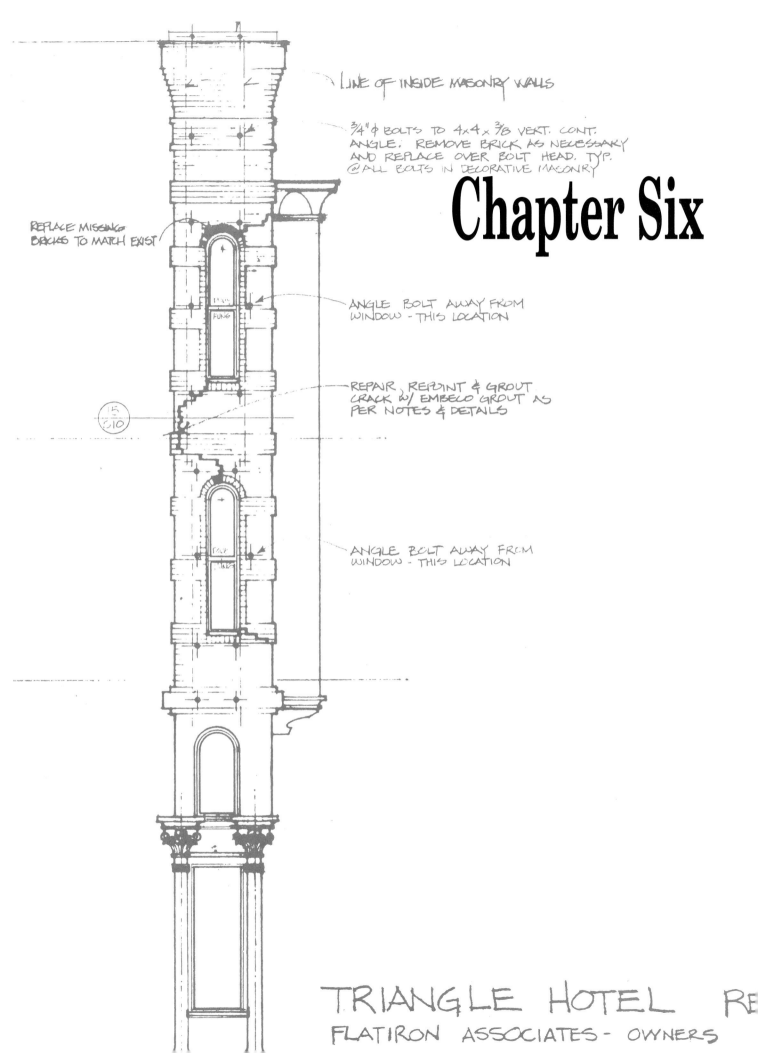

LINE OF INSIDE MASONRY WALLS

3/4"∅ BOLTS TO 4x4x3/8 VERT. CONT.
ANGLE: REMOVE BRICK AS NECESSARY
AND REPLACE OVER BOLT HEAD. TYP.
@ALL BOLTS IN DECORATIVE MASONRY

Chapter Six

REPLACE MISSING
BRICKS TO MATCH EXIST.

ANGLE BOLT AWAY FROM
WINDOW - THIS LOCATION

REPAIR, REPOINT & GROUT
CRACK W/ EMBECO GROUT AS
PER NOTES & DETAILS

ANGLE BOLT AWAY FROM
WINDOW - THIS LOCATION

TRIANGLE HOTEL RE

FLATIRON ASSOCIATES - OWNERS

Merchants on Main Street

In the late nineteenth century, commerce was the lifeblood of a community, and the number of stores and shops standing along Main Street were vital signs of civic health. Even a town's familiar gridiron street plan was designed to entice prospective merchants with conveniently sized lots and prominent corner locations.

The first shops on Main Street, however, were a far cry from the retail emporia of which boosters dreamed. The early general store was a simple structure (usually of frame construction, but sometimes built of logs), and its stock and merchandise were limited to whatever could be

Riverside Avenue
Fire swept through many Washington cities in the late nineteenth and early twentieth centuries, reducing countless frame structures to ashes. But the devastation had one positive result: it cleared the way for new business centers, regulated by strict fire codes and characterized by buildings of brick and stone. Nowhere was the transformation more dramatic than in Spokane, where an 1889 fire levelled downtown businesses and forced merchants into tents and makeshift shacks. Within the year, however, multistoried brick buildings rose up phoenix-like from the debris. By the early twentieth century, Riverside Avenue (shown in this photograph from about 1920) boasted an unsurpassed collection of commercial towers: including the majestic Old National Bank building (rear, left side), 1911, designed by Daniel Burnham, America's preeminent commercial architect of the period; and the Sherwood building of 1916-1917 (foreground, left side), designed by Spokane's Cutter and Malmgren. On the right side of the street are (from front to rear) the Fernwell and Paulsen buildings, which still stand. (Fernwell Building, National Register; all others, State Inventory)

Oxford Tavern
Built in 1900 in Snohomish, the Oxford Tavern is an ornate example of a false front or "boomtown" building. The cast iron columns, bracketed tin cornice, and large plate glass windows create a sophisticated facade for the simple frame structure. (National Register)

brought in by steamer, schooner, stage, or packtrain. Some pioneer entrepreneurs offered more specialized services—barbers and blacksmiths, for example—but the general store was a community's economic mainstay. Most of these early commercial enterprises disappeared long ago, but a few towns never outgrew them. Today, the Richardson Store on Lopez Island and the Cloverland Store in Asotin County are reminders of these simple shops of the past.

As towns grew and the regional economy matured, general stores were replaced by a wide range of commercial establishments. By the 1870s, most towns hoped to boast as Olympia did that the "principal stores keep a fine assortment of goods and of a character to suit all classes of people. A well established bank is also located in the city, and travellers will find the hotels comfortable." After all, as a Seattle writer noted in the same decade, "the status of a town can be accurately ascertained by the appearance of its places of business."

Appearance was important indeed, and, by the 1870s, the main streets of a score of Washington communities were lined with frame structures boasting lofty "false front" facades. The high parapet of the typical false front building blocked from view the rather simple structure behind it, and gave to

what otherwise was a modest building an urbane sense of size and style. From Walla Walla to Olympia, false fronts were ornamented with bracketed cornices and elaborate window hoods, reflecting the influence of the Italianate style, which at that time was popular in the business centers of the East and Midwest.

The false front was the quintessential architectural expression of the pioneer boomtown, and its pretentiousness sometimes outstripped reality, just as the civic booster's inflated dreams and hopes for a community often were an exercise in self delusion. As cities grew, these structures gradually passed from the scene, but in smaller communities false fronts were still being constructed well into the twentieth century, examples of which yet can be seen on the main streets of LaConner, Coupeville, Snohomish, and other small towns both east and west of the Cascades.

Many false front buildings were destroyed by the frequent fires that swept through mercantile centers in this era. In the statehood year of 1889 alone, fire ravaged the commercial districts of Seattle, Spokane, Ellensburg, Roslyn, and Vancouver destroying hundreds of frame structures and forcing merchants into tents.

Port Townsend Business Block

In a typical business block, such as the Tibbals Block in Port Townsend, several businesses occupied a single large building. Usually, storefront retail shops were situated on the street level; doctor's and lawyer's offices were located on the second story; and a fraternal hall filled the upper level. (Port Townsend Historic District, National Register and National Historic Landmark)

Starbuck Bank
Neoclassical imagery was utilized in the facades of even the smallest banks to convey a sense of solidity, tradition, and security. Though diminutive, the Starbuck Bank in Columbia County is a dignified structure. The bank, built in 1903, is embellished with arched openings and a projecting cornice. (National Register)

Meanwhile, city councils hastily enacted strict fire codes. Even in the early twentieth century, large conflagrations remained a threat; in 1903, twenty-two blocks of Aberdeen burned, and, in 1909, downtown Wenatchee was engulfed by flames.

As local newspaper editors were quick to note, these fires allowed towns to improve their business centers by recasting entire commercial blocks in brick and stone. Within a few years, imposing rows of contiguous masonry

buildings arose from the ashes, complete with decorative metal cornices, great plate glass display windows, and cast-iron storefront columns.

The business districts in Spokane and Seattle were expanded and rebuilt on a far grander scale, but even in small communities, such as Waterville, the burnt-out wooden buildings were replaced by uniform rows of brick buildings sharing party walls. No one could deny that towns like these were back in business, and, architecturally at least, they were bigger and better than ever.

Fire alone, of course, did not reshape the physical appearance of commercial districts; energetic promoters and developers, and continued economic growth, played major roles as well. The seaport towns of Fairhaven and Port Townsend, for instance, each had some of the most impressive business districts in the state in the 1890s, with multistoried masonry buildings built by investors who hoped to turn these cities into great trade and transportation centers. Developers also established a substantial commercial center in Everett in anticipation of a growing industrial-based economy in that community. The Klondike gold rush spurred commercial growth in Seattle after 1897. Elsewhere west of the Cascades, logging, sawmilling, and railroad expansion encouraged the establishment of other commercial centers on Puget Sound and in southwestern Washington.

East of the mountains, a rich agricultural hinterland supported booming commercial centers. The business districts of Ellensburg, Colfax, and Waitsburg, for example, were enriched by the trade of surrounding ranchers, orchardists, and, especially, wheat farmers. Regional gold strikes and other mining activity led to a brisk business in outfitting prospectors and mine developers at Walla Walla in the 1860s (for the Idaho and Montana gold strikes) and Spokane in the 1880s-1890s (northern Idaho silver mining).

But the greatest impetus for creating new towns and cities was the railroad. In the early 1880s, railroad towns from Spokane and Ritzville to Pasco and North Yakima (now Yakima) sprang up practically overnight once the tracks arrived. In fact, even the faintest hint of laying down rails could precipitate an overnight boom, as investors and developers poured thousands of dollars into a community's proposed commercial district.

Across the state, the characteristic building seen in these bustling new trade centers was the "business block," usually a substantial edifice of "fireproof" brick that spanned several lots, stood two or more stories high, and contained a wide variety of commercial services. Business blocks usually housed retail shops on the ground floor, and offices, apartments, or meeting halls on the upper floors. If the "false front" of the 1870s and 1880s marked the beginning of a boomtown's economy, then the "business blocks" of the next decade offered solid evidence that a community's commercial center had truly come of age.

Citadels of Trade in the Age of Rail

The arrival of the first transcontinental railroads in the 1880s assured a bright future for Spokane, Tacoma, Seattle, Yakima, and Vancouver. As hubs in a vast rail system, they were destined to experience a surge in mercantile, financial, and social growth. For towns and villages bypassed by the tracks, the future was not nearly so bright; communities without rail connections had difficulty in just surviving.

Railroads, of course, exerted a powerful influence on the development of regional commerce, and new branch lines facilitated trade in practically every inhabited part of the state. But just as importantly, railways concentrated commercial activity in regional centers. The commercial hearts of these communities, particularly Tacoma, Seattle, Spokane, and Yakima, grew dense with impressive buildings, vast warehouses, and "commercial blocks."

Smith Tower
By the early 1900s, skyscrapers were changing the silhouettes of cities. The invention of the elevator created exciting possibilities for high rise construction. And, with the use of reinforced steel for the skeletal framework (shown here in a 1914 photo of the Smith Tower in Seattle's Pioneer Square), architects were able to maximize floor and window space, and express the "bones" of a building. (National Register)

The railroad right-of-way never was far from sight, and usually ran straight through the business district. In Centralia, for example, the "hub city" of southwestern Washington, the commercial center assumed a typically linear form down Tower Avenue, paralleling the tracks and yarding area.

Commerce in the railroad age was conducted in substantial Renaissance or Romanesque Revival buildings that conveyed a sense of solidity and strength. Standing as high as five stories, they exhibited arched windows, decorative cornices, and the names of the owners prominently engraved or embossed on the parapets.

As Seattle and Spokane rebuilt after the great fires of 1889, their new mercantile districts featured scores of these grand buildings, some of which were among the most impressive in the entire West. Elmer Fisher, one of the state's first architects, designed a series of Romanesque Revival style structures in Seattle, thereby helping to introduce a new, expanded scale to the commercial heart of the rebuilt city. One of the finest examples of his work was the Pioneer Building (1889-1890), owned by the prominent Seattle developer Henry Yesler. The massive arched entryway, made of rough-faced stone, gave muscular visual expression to the grandiose ambitions of the young city. John Parkinson's Interurban Building

(1890) and Albert Wickersham's Maynard Building (1892) were equally impressive with their soaring brick piers and monumental arches; both were well-designed versions of the commercial idiom popularized by the nationally famous architect H. H. Richardson. In Tacoma, architects Heath and Gove, and Carl Darmer, designed a number of commercial blocks in both the Romanesque and Renaissance Revival modes, as did Herman Preusse, J. K. Dow, C. B. Seaton, and C. Ferris White in Spokane.

Economic Expansion in the New Century

At the turn of the century, commercial districts continued to grow. The regrading of downtown Seattle allowed businesses to expand beyond the confines of Pioneer Square. In quick succession, financial and retail districts and a public market were developed north of the older business center. In Tacoma, a series of warehouses spread south from the depot, and in Yakima new businesses were built east of the original Front Street district. As commerce expanded and diversified, new materials were used in commercial architecture including terra-cotta, reinforced steel, and concrete.

No building typified the new commercial age better than the warehouse,

Cloverland Garage

Built in 1902, Howard's Hall was a kind of community center for the small eastern Washington town of Cloverland. The street level housed the Florence and Company general merchandise store. Upstairs was Howard's Dance Hall. In 1904, the first telephone service in Asotin County was established with offices in this building. Later, a post office was located here. In 1918, three years after the first automobile came to Cloverland, the building was converted into a garage and continued to function as such through the 1930s. During that time, the upstairs was used as a dormitory for school children unable to travel home due to winter storms. Today, practically nothing remains of Cloverland, except this structure. (National Register)

Tacoma
Warehouse District
Wherever railroads ran
through urban centers,
warehouse districts
grew up closeby.
Tacoma's warehouse
buildings, erected in
the late nineteenth and
early twentieth
centuries, exhibited a
simple straightforward
style that emphasized
function over
ornamentation.
(National Register)

which served as a receiving and distribution point for a never ending stream
of manufactured goods arriving by
train. Warehouse design largely was
determined by functional concerns,
mainly the need for large open interiors
within a structural framework that
could support heavy loads. Exterior
design usually was a straightforward
composition of piers and spandrels.
Many warehouses were capped by
classical cornices, suggesting the
importance of these storehouses in the
new commercial age. The most imposing group of warehouses in the state
stood near Tacoma's Union Depot,
where rows of impressive masonry
structures handled goods in a region-
wide distribution system.

Much of this merchandise ended
up on the shelves of the numerous
department stores built in the early
years of the century. These retail
emporia offered, under one roof, all of
the products of an emerging consumer
society— hardware, clothing, furniture,
notions, even foodstuffs. The largest
included the Bon Marche and Frederick
and Nelson stores in Seattle, and the
Crescent in Spokane, but family-owned
department stores were located in
nearly every sizeable community.

Architects designed these multistoried buildings with open interiors
and expansive windows for lighting and
display. At its finest, the department

store was a kind of Neoclassical or Renaissance palace, ornamented like the J. S. Graham store (1919) in Seattle, with ornate terra-cotta. Inside, many of the stores featured massive columns, capped with classical capitals, as if to suggest that these were the palazzi of modern-day de'Medici merchants.

Among the most imposing structures in any commercial district were the banks, which invariably exhibited architectural designs that set them apart from neighboring businesses. Even the most mundane Main Street had a Classical Revival styled bank, with pedimented facade, portico, and monumental cornice. The imagery, of course, was clear—it was a showy testimonial to the institution's reputed financial soundness and strength. It was the style adopted all across Washington from the diminutive Bank of Starbuck, built in 1903, to Tacoma's impressive Bank of California, constructed just before the Great Depression.

For travelers, of course, a commercial center often was judged by the quality of its hotels. In earlier decades, Washington's hotels were little more than boarding houses, but the coming of the railroads changed that forever. Trains brought an influx of visitors in numbers unimaginable a few years before. Salesmen, investors, job seekers, purchasing agents, vacationers, and home seekers all arrived by train on a regular basis, and, to accommodate these guests, hotels were built in record numbers.

Many hotels were relatively plain, having rooms with neither running water nor a view. But others were magnificent destination points in themselves and were symbols of civic pride. Perhaps no hotel in the state was more renowned than Spokane's Davenport Hotel, designed by Kirtland Cutter in a Renaissance Revival mode and acclaimed as the finest in the West.

Even relatively modest inns, such as the Waterville Hotel (1907), were hailed by town fathers as centers of urbane social life and harbingers of coming prosperity. When individual entrepreneurs did not step forward to fund a grand hotel, then the business community often united to undertake the effort. This occurred in Olympia with the building of the Hotel Olympian (1924), and in Seattle with the construction of the Olympic Hotel (1924-1929), designed by America's foremost hotel architect, George B. Post.

By the early twentieth century, central business districts had grown so dense that expansion could only go skyward. In fact, towering new office buildings were replacing the church steeple and courthouse dome as the most imposing landmarks on

Davenport Hotel
Designed by noted architect Kirtland Cutter, Spokane's Davenport Hotel was a phenomenon of the railroad era. In this period, the grandest hotels provided not only lodging, but also were locations for social events, dances, receptions, and civic meetings. Built in several phases between 1901 and 1914, the Davenport was considered to be the grandest hostelry in the Northwest. (National Register)

Washington's urban skylines. The development of steel frame construction techniques and the introduction of the elevator made the modern skyscraper possible. The Alaska Building was Washington's first steel frame skyscraper—a brick and terra-cotta clad structure that rose fourteen stories above Seattle's Second Avenue. In 1911, Daniel Burnham of Chicago, America's leading commercial architect, designed the Old National Bank Building in Spokane, a steel frame skyscraper with Renaissance Revival details. In 1916-1917, Kirtland Cutter designed the nearby Sherwood Building, faced in terra-cotta with arched windows reminiscent of the Gothic Revival style.

But the most distinguished early skyscraper in the state was the Smith Tower in Seattle. Financed and built in 1914 by an eastern industrialist, the Smith Tower was the tallest building in the West when completed, and remained the highest in Washington for several decades. It was a remarkable architectural statement for its day—a frankly expressed steel frame, faced in gleaming terra-cotta, and crowned with a pyramidal cap.

Generally, skyscrapers such as the Smith Tower and the Old National Bank adhered to a classical design vocabulary, in which the building was a metaphor for an ancient Greek column, with a ground-floor base, a shaft of office floors, and a crowning capital. But if the decorative imagery had historical antecedents, the structural system was thoroughly modern. Exterior walls were reduced to the framing elements, and located between the piers were wide windows, allowing ample light and ventilation for the honeycomb of offices inside.

By the 1920s, architects played with setbacks and sculpted profiles. The best of this era included the Art Deco styled Northern Life Tower (1928-1929) in Seattle designed by A. H. Albertson, the Medical Arts Building

(1930) in Tacoma by John Graham, and the Larson Building (1931) in Yakima by John Maloney. But these were among the last large-scale commercial structures to be built for many years. With the onset of the depression in the early 1930s, construction activity in business districts came to a virtual halt.

Throughout this era, astute observers sensed a kind of anarchy in the layout of the state's commercial centers, where a wide variety of structural styles and types were haphazardly intermixed. In fact, little effort had ever been taken to impose any design coherence in growing cities. One notable exception, however, was the never completed City Beautiful plans developed by Howells and Stokes for the Metropolitan Tract in downtown Seattle. This area eventually did include some handsome office buildings, including the classically inspired Cobb Building (1910) by Howell and Stokes, and the Skinner Building (1926) by Robert Reamer. The planned industrial community of Longview, dating from the early 1920s, imposed strict height limits and design guidelines for businesses along Commerce Avenue. Such efforts at planning, however, were exceptions and held little appeal for modern businessmen.

Northern Life Tower
Seattle's Northern Life Tower, designed by A. H. Albertson and built in 1928-1929, is one of the state's finest examples of the Modernistic or Art Deco style. Reportedly, the building was inspired by the reflection of Mount Rainier in Lake Washington and reflects the colors of this scenery in the dark to light hues of the exterior brickwork. (National Register)

Teapot Dome
The Teapot Dome gas station, built in 1922 on US Route 12 near Zillah, is an outstanding example of roadway novelty architecture of the era. The building is a humorous reminder of the Teapot Dome oil scandal of the Harding administration, intending to catch the attention of passing motorists. (National Register)

The Automobile and Highway Commerce

More than anything else, the automobile revolutionized life in modern America. Just as the railroads had reshaped commercial development in the late nineteenth century, the appearance of cars and trucks had a dramatic effect on Washington's businesses in the twentieth century.

By the 1910s, newly constructed ribbons of concrete and gravel for cars and trucks began radiating out from the state's population hubs. Almost from the beginning, small-scale retailers set up businesses alongside highways to serve motorists and a growing suburban population. For the most part, merchants operated grocery stores, gas stations, restaurants, and motor hotels (soon shortened to "motels"), or a combination of these, such as Keeler's Korner on the Pacific Highway between Seattle and Everett.

Not surprisingly, new architectural forms were developed to serve this budding highway commerce. Typically, these buildings were low, freestanding structures that bore little relationship to their environment and exhibited few decorative elements. Instead, merchants erected bold signs to capture the fancy of the passing drivers, and a portion of each commercial lot was turned into parking space.

A notable exception to the relative blandness of highway architecture was the "novelty" building, which humorously enlisted architecture to create structures that were themselves larger-than-life billboards promoting the business housed within. Examples in Washington ranged from the Benewah Dairy's milk-bottle shaped shops in Spokane, to the Teapot Dome service station near Zillah.

The trend toward the suburbanization of commerce culminated with the development of large regional shopping centers that invariably stood alongside major roadways. The Northgate Shopping Center (1950) in Seattle was among the first in the country and a prototype that was adopted nationwide. These centers, with their excellent parking facilities, made shopping easier and quickly proliferated throughout the Pacific Northwest.

Inevitably, the establishment of suburban malls precipitated the decline of many traditional downtown business districts, which, after all, had been designed to serve a population dependent on rail transportation and the horse and buggy. Ever since the coming of the automobile, in fact, congestion in city streets and a lack of adequate parking space have remained endemic problems in core urban areas. Today, numerous buildings and office spaces stand empty in old commercial districts in both town and city, because local merchants have relocated in shopping malls. The traditional commercial centers of the largest cities, including Seattle and Spokane, generally have fared better due to mass transportation facilities and a commitment by the business community to remain downtown.

Washington.
State Normal.
SCHOOL.
Ellensburgh. Wash.
E. C. Price. Arch't

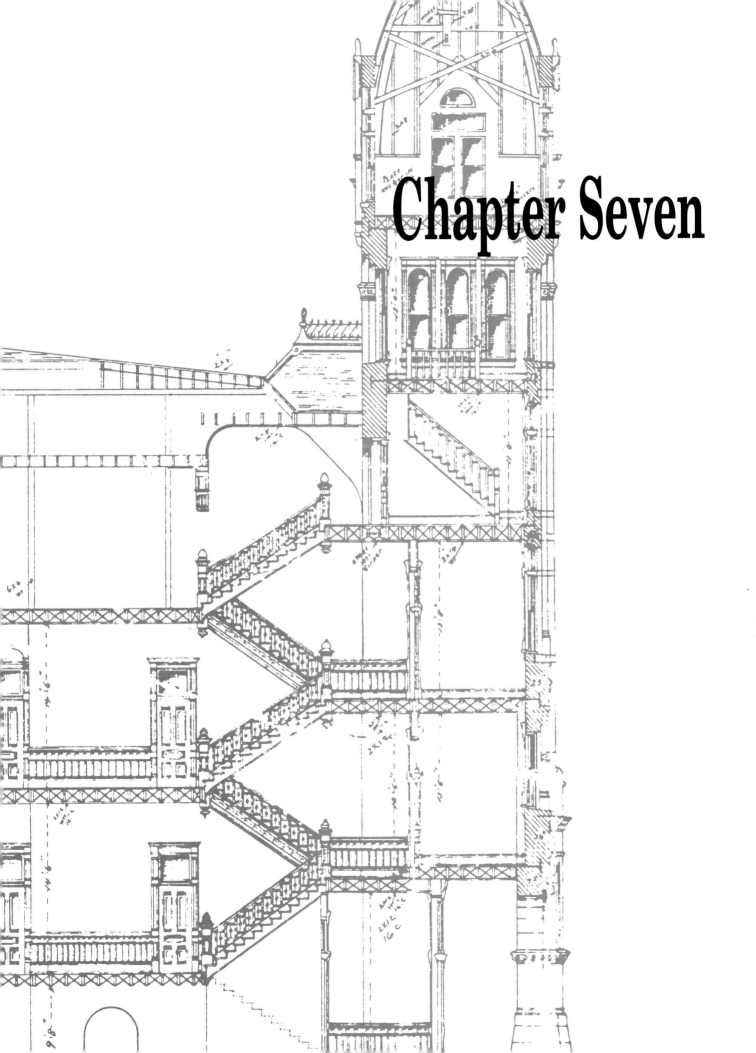

Chapter Seven

Foundations of the Community

Communities are groupings of structures inhabited by residents who are united by common residence. As such, communities convey a sense of place, and define in many ways who we are as a people. Certain buildings in particular bond citizens together, mainly schools, social clubs, meeting halls, churches, granges, city halls, and various other governmental and community facilities.

The demand at the local level for governmental, judicial, fire, and police services grew as Washington evolved from a territory into a state. Obviously, when county and town governments formed, one of their first duties was

Holy Trinity Orthodox Church
Built at the turn of the century by immigrant miners from eastern Europe, the Holy Trinity Orthodox Church in Wilkeson is the oldest Orthodox church in Washington. Slavic coal miners and their families raised funds, contributed labor, and provided many of the icons and furnishings. Outwardly, it is a simple frame country church, except for the unique "onion" dome. Inside, the Carpathian-Ukranian style iconography is typical of the traditional Orthodox faith and is believed to have been imported from Czarist Russia. Only a few wooden benches line the inside walls, since the congregation remains standing during worship services. Dating from about 1898, Holy Trinity continues to serve the Orthodox religious community. (National Register)

**Garfield
County Courthouse**
Built in 1901,
Pomeroy's Garfield
County Courthouse is
one of a number of
elaborate courthouses
constructed at the turn
of the century. Its
prominent setting and
ornate design are
reflective of the
importance of local
government at a time
when Washington was
making the transition
from frontier conditions
into the modern age.
(National Register)

to provide buildings from which to conduct basic administrative duties, public safety, and a judicial system.

New city halls and courthouses, which in the early days usually housed all of a community's governmental activities under one roof, immediately became focal points of community life. The impressive architecture, expensive construction materials, and prominent location of many courthouses and city halls further enhanced their significance to the community. The Garfield County Courthouse in Pomeroy and the Spokane County Courthouse in Spokane are just two marvelous examples of these grand structures.

Naturally, as a city or town grew, so did the size and diversity of its governmental and public service agencies, which no longer could all be maintained in a single building or even a couple of structures. Consequently, specialized facilities appeared, such as fire stations, street department garages, and police stations, which, of course, have become familiar landmarks in any urban scene. In the largest cities, separate fire and police stations were situated to serve different neighborhoods. A particularly interesting example is the Wallingford Fire and Police Station, located in a Seattle residential neighborhood. The station's modified saltbox design and the materials used in its construction were intentionally utilized to harmonize with the surrounding Craftsman and bungalow style houses.

Schools and Colleges

Early pioneers insisted that their children receive a basic education, and they established schools as soon as a teacher could be found, who often as not was the mother of one or more of the pupils. Classes gathered wherever shelter could be provided, most frequently in a settler's barn or cabin. A few years later came the hiring of a school teacher and the erection of a one-room schoolhouse, which usually was one of the first public buildings to go up in a community.

Throughout the late nineteenth and early twentieth centuries, thousands of small schoolhouses dotted Washington's rural and urban landscape. Unfortunately, most now are gone, and, of those that remain, few are in a good state of preservation. The Blue Mountain School, located in the foothills of the Olympic Mountains in Clallam County, is one fine existing example of this kind of school. It is a typical one-room, gable roofed, wood-framed structure.

Until 1895, public schools were funded and supported locally, resulting in great disparities in the type of facili-

ties and quality of instruction between various school districts. In that year, however, the Washington legislature passed the "Barefoot Schoolboy Law" authorizing state support for all public schools, resulting in a uniformity of curriculum and higher standards in all of Washington's classrooms.

In this period, more substantial school buildings became common and they were pointed to with pride by residents of small rural crossroads and large city neighborhoods alike. Washington's great population boom, continuing through the 1890s and into the early decades of the twentieth

Wallingford Fire Station
As cities grew, individual neighborhoods were assigned their own public service facilities. In 1913, this police and fire station was built to serve the residents of Seattle's Wallingford district. Designed by city architect Daniel R. Huntington to house equestrian police patrols and horse drawn fire equipment, the structure was intended to blend in harmoniously with Wallingford's bungalows and Craftsman style houses. (National Register)

century, affected educational facilities in a significant way. More children meant larger schools, and pupils began attending classes for longer hours and for more years. As the curriculum expanded, auditoriums, laboratories, and gymnasiums were incorporated into these new structures in addition to classrooms and offices.

In the early 1890s, there were only three recognized four-year high schools in the entire state, but, by the early twentieth century, scores of high schools flourished, particularly in the state's larger communities. Spokane's Lewis and Clark High School, constructed in 1912 in an imposing Gothic Revival style, was one of these early educational institutions. With its strikingly ornate facade and standing in a prominent location close to the heart of the city, it has long served as a reminder of Spokane's strong commitment to public education.

The first public institution of higher education, the University of Washington, was authorized by the territorial legislature in 1861, and opened that year in Seattle with one instructor and one collegiate student. Originally located close to the old downtown area, the college mostly floundered in bankruptcy and disinterest for three decades, until moved to its present location near Lake Washington in 1895 when a strong new beginning was instituted.

In 1890, the legislature also authorized what are now Washington State University in Pullman, Eastern Washington University at Cheney, and Central Washington University of Ellensburg. Western Washington University in Bellingham was founded three years later. Numerous private colleges and academies likewise were established in Washington, beginning with Walla Walla's Whitman College dating from 1859.

These campuses retain many architecturally significant buildings that played critical roles in the history of each institution. Eastern Washington University's administration building, Showalter Hall, is a good example of a building originally intended to house an entire college—classrooms, laboratories, offices, dormitory, etc. As the college grew, academic departments and services moved into new buildings, while Showalter Hall, with its outstanding Renaissance design, remained as the administrative center and hub of the expanding campus complex.

In Pullman, Thompson Hall likewise played a central role in the development of Washington State University, the state's major land-grant college. Dedicated in 1895 (and originally known as the Administration Building), Thompson Hall was the symbol for a revitalized second beginning for the institution after it had survived a period of great turmoil in the early 1890s. In addition to serious monetary and administrative squabbles, two presidents had been sacked, and opponents from other communities had assaulted the institution in the hope that it would fail and be relocated elsewhere by the legislature.

Churches and Religious Institutions

By the 1840s, missionaries were proselytizing to Native Americans in wilderness encampments and ministering to fur traders at Hudson's Bay Company posts. After mid century, the increasing numbers of American immigrants and the growth of towns led to the building of churches and the acquiring of resident priests and ministers. As with erecting a school, the construction of a church was a significant accomplishment on the raw frontier. Frequently, the structure functioned as school and meeting hall as well as church, and therefore assumed the central role in community life.

An outstanding example of a church from Washington's early territorial era still stands on a wooded hill in the tiny village of Claquato near Chehalis. Built in 1858, this small yet dignified structure was constructed with whipsawed boards and exhibits

Blue Mountain School Located in the northern foothills of the Olympic mountains just west of Port Angeles, the Blue Mountain School typified the strong link that existed between educational and community activities in a remote region. The simple one-room structure, built in 1903, served as a school and as a location for social gatherings and civic meetings. (National Register)

Japanese Language School

Tacoma's Japanese Language School, or Nihon Go Gakko, was established in 1911 in the home of its founder and first teacher, Kuni Yamasaki. In about 1922, parents, local residents, and the Japanese Association raised funds to build a permanent structure, which was expanded in 1927. In concept and function, the school provided instruction in the culture and traditions of Japan, including ethical principles and values. As many as 200 students spent nearly two hours daily after public school and three to four hours every Saturday receiving instruction. The school was a stabilizing element in the community—a place where newcomers could learn English, meet their neighbors, and participate in social activities. Though architecturally nondescript, the school was a focal point for what was, until World War II, the largest Japanese neighborhood in the state. During the wartime removal of all west coast Japanese-Americans in 1942, Japanese residents were ordered to report to the school for registration, subsequent to evacuation to internment camps. (National Register)

Claquato Church

This small church is the most noteworthy remnant of Claquato, an early Lewis County village located near Chehalis. Dating from 1858, it is one of the last remaining Washington territorial churches. The simple Greek Revival structure was built with lumber donated by Lewis H. Davis, the earliest settler in the town. Nails were fabricated by a local blacksmith, and the pews and pulpit were donated by other settlers. A symbolic crown of thorns adorns the upper octagonal portion of the belfry. In 1953, a major renovation project directed by a local American Legion post restored the church to its original condition. (National Register)

Greek Revival design elements. Its symmetrical composition is capped by a belfry mounted with a symbolic crown of thorns. It retains its original windows, central door, returned cornices, and corner pilasters.

Following the completion of the first transcontinental railroads in the 1880s, larger and more elaborate churches were constructed as Washington's population and wealth grew by great bounds. Founded in 1879, the Westminster Congregational Church of Spokane is that city's oldest congregation of any denomination, and traces its lineage to the missionary work of Cushing Eells beginning in 1838. The congregation's rough-cut granite building was built in 1890, after the city's great fire destroyed all existing churches. Gothic in detail, with hints of the Romanesque Revival style in its massing, Westminster set the architectural standard for subsequent churches built in Spokane and the Inland Empire.

By the turn of the century, Washington increasingly was the destination for European immigrants arriving by rail from the East and Midwest. Thousands stepped off trains in urban areas and at rural junctions seeking the good land and jobs promised in the promotional literature distributed far and wide by railroad propagandists. Coming as they were into an unfamiliar cultural setting and environment, the church served as a stabilizing element for Norwegian, German, Swedish, and other immigrants. For a period of time, the local pastor remained a dominant leader for the close-knit ethnic community.

Polish immigrants arrived in the Chehalis River Valley of western Lewis County in the 1880s to work in the forests and sawmills. By 1892, the Polish community formed a Roman Catholic parish known as St. Joseph's, located at Pe Ell. When a pastor who was not Polish was appointed to St. Joseph's, discontented parishioners eventually broke away from the mainstream Catholic Church to form their own parish of the Polish National Catholic Church (PNCC) in America. With volunteer labor and donated materials, the Holy Cross PNCC was completed in 1916 in a vernacular Gothic Revival style. At Holy Cross, the Polish congregation worshipped in their traditional style and in their native tongue. Today, the edifice looks much as it did in 1916, and is one of very few Polish National Catholic Churches yet remaining in the western United States.

Spokane's Holy Trinity Greek Orthodox Church, erected in 1948 and supplementing an adjacent Greek community hall built earlier in 1933, might look more at home in Athens, Greece,

Slavonian Hall
Tacoma's Slavonian Hall was built as a meetinghouse and social hall for the Slavonian-American Benevolent Society. Constructed in 1902, it served the financial, social, and cultural needs of many eastern European immigrants who settled in the Tacoma area. (National Register)

than on the city's Washington Street. The structure's squarish domed mass is distinguished by horizontal banding of red and white brick, and by two polygonal towers. The impressive interior is highlighted by dazzling artwork executed in gold leaf.

Societies, Clubs, and Community Halls

Along with educational, governmental, and religious institutions, social organizations have been instrumental in bonding individuals together in a community. The early pioneers often retained their affiliation with the Masons, the Grand Army of the Republic (GAR), or other clubs and organizations that they had belonged to in the east, and, of course, they often started other new organizations. In territorial times, club and fraternal meetings commonly were held in family kitchens, saloons, or general stores. New schools, town halls, churches, and courthouses likewise provided meeting space for the growing number of lodges, women's leagues, temperance societies, and service clubs.

By the late nineteenth century, many organizations began constructing their own facilities. For instance, the Farmington Masonic Hall was a typical fraternal lodge in a small, rural eastern Washington town near the Idaho line. Farmington's Masons organized in

Masonic Temple

This Masonic Temple is included in Spokane's Riverside Avenue Historic District. It was originally designed in 1904 by Loren L. Rand, but increasing membership in the early 1920s necessitated expanding and remodeling the original structure. The expansion utilizes transitional architectural elements that link the original Beaux Arts design with a more restrained classicism. The present facility now accommodates some twenty-three Masonic organizations, as well as occasional community activities. (National Register)

Redmen Lodge
Redmen Hall is one
of several buildings
comprising the
Skamokawa Historic
District. Designed by
the Portland architect
Allen Riley, the building
was used as a school
until 1926 when it
became a meeting hall
for the Redmen
fraternal organization.
Recently, the "Friends
of Skamokawa" have
rallied support to
restore the building to
its original condition.
(National Register)

1906, and, after fire destroyed the first lodge, the group constructed the existing modest, two-story, wood-frame building in 1908. Typically, volunteer labor built the structure, which remained in use by the Masons until 1985. Its present utilization as a community center still underscores the historic importance of the building to the community.

Foreign immigrants likewise formed their own social organizations. By the early twentieth century, Swedes, Finns, Poles, Austro-Croatians, and Chinese all had established ethnic neighborhoods in the bustling Grays Harbor port cities of Aberdeen, Hoquiam, and Cosmopolis. Neighborhood life revolved around the ethnically oriented lodges and halls, where a variety of educational, social, cultural, and political activities took place.

The Finnish Brotherhood Association Hall, which played a key role in the social and political life of Aberdeen's Finns for eighty years, is one of the best preserved ethnic social clubs in Washington. Built in 1902 and tucked away on Randall Street, it housed the Finnish public library and was the scene of plays, musicals, rallies, and celebrations. Meetings were conducted in Finnish until 1976.

In rural areas, chapters of the Washington State Grange sponsored social, cultural, and educational activities. The Grange also was politically active, effectively wielding influence at county courthouses and in the Olympia statehouse. Many unassuming grange halls were erected in agricultural localities from the turn of the century up to the 1920s. A number of them still stand today, though usually in altered or dilapidated condition.

By the early 1900s, fraternal and service organizations had grown to the extent that they were able to construct impressive lodges at prominent downtown locations. The Naval Lodge Elks building, erected in 1927 in Port Angeles, is typical of these elaborate clubs. Designed by Seattle architect J. Charles Stanley, the structure's facade sported Renaissance Revival detailing and decorative exterior brickwork. Inside were meeting rooms, overnight accommodations, a swimming pool, and retail space on the ground floor. The facility served not only Elk members, but other Clallam County residents as well by hosting various community events and activities. Today, the five-story building remains as the city's tallest structure.

Chapter Eight

RECONSTRUCTION OF
THE CAPITOL THEATRE
11 SOUTH THIRD STREET
YAKIMA, WASHINGTON
FOR THE
CITY OF YAKIMA

SHEET

A
5

DATE

PADDOCK & HOLLINGBERY Architects
YAKIMA, WASH. — MOSES LAKE, WASH.
A.I.A.
31
OCT
77

Washington at Play

Imagine, if you will, Washingtonians at leisure and play in the past. In the 1880s, loggers pack into a wood frame structure and watch with stunned silence as a powdered and rouged actor, dressed in crimson velvet, recites lines from Macbeth. At Seattle's 1909 Alaska-Yukon-Pacific Exposition, children squeal with delight while riding the new ferris wheel. In the 1780s, two Indian riders on horseback strain to gain the lead as they round the last curve on a racetrack marked out in a wilderness meadow.

Washington's history is rich with the evidence that the first inhabitants entertained themselves with their

Natatorium Carousel

The magnificent carousel in Spokane's Riverside Park is a wondrous machine that has provided entertainment for generations. Carved in 1909, the merry-go-round was a wedding gift from master carver Charles I. Looff to his daughter, Emma. Loof's daughter and son-in-law operated the carousel in Spokane's old Natatorium Park. The carousel features fifty-four leaping horses. Each hand carved animal is adorned with flowers, parrots, cupids, or clusters of fruit—colorful details that enhance each animal's individuality. It is estimated that nearly 100,000 people a year have ridden the smiling wooden steeds since the carousel was relocated to Riverside Park for Expo 74. (National Register)

Capitol Theater
Yakima's Capitol
Theater (originally
named the Mercy
Theater and later the
Lowe State Theater)
was designed in 1920
by B. Marcus Priteca.
Commissioned by
Frederick Mercy, it was
intended to be the
largest and best
combination (motion
picture, vaudeville, and
road show) theater in
the West. The exterior
adheres to classical
design elements, with
a facade of terra-cotta
and patterned
brickwork. The interior
exhibits the opulence
typical of the best
theaters built in the
1920s. (National
Register)

own pastimes. At Old Man House in Suquamish, for instance, archaeologists have discovered bone pieces from a game still played by Native Americans today. These artifacts, and such sites as the historic Chenquoss Indian race-track in Skamania County, tell us that Native Americans found time to devise contests and establish locations for their leisurely pursuits.

To be sure, the early immigrants clustered in and around Washington's first frontier communities also indulged in amusements, as do their descendants today. Identifying the historic buildings, structures, and sites associated with entertainment can provide valuable insight into the significant role that recreation played in the lives of nineteenth- and twentieth-century Washingtonians.

Theaters and Movie Houses

Performance halls, opera houses, theaters, and the like have, over the years, changed in design and function as the entertainment business has evolved. Early theatrical performances were held in any building with a large enough room to accommodate a crowd, such as a saloon, school, or general store. Second-story fraternal meeting rooms, located above ground-floor commercial enterprises, frequently were utilized for this purpose. In these halls, paying customers walked up a narrow

Naches Bandstand
As in many small towns, the Naches bandstand was an object of civic pride and an activity center for the community. Constructed about 1919 by the Naches Commercial Club with labor, funds, and materials donated by local residents, the bandstand was a project that involved the entire community. This podium continues to provide a platform for local politicians, musicians, and civic rallies. (National Register)

back stairway and into a large rectangular space crammed with folding chairs.

As stage productions gained in popularity and frequency, new theaters and performance halls followed. The Moore Theater in Seattle is an excellent example of an early building constructed specifically for presenting live entertainment. The popular stars of the vaudeville circuit performed on its opulent stage. Its interior, virtually unchanged today from when it opened in 1907, is richly appointed in a classical motif with Italian marble and brass. It is one of very few of the once numerous vaudevillian theaters to remain intact.

The advent of celluloid in the early twentieth century offered spectators a wider variety of visual entertainment. Nickelodeon theaters were small, simply built structures, often sandwiched between other commercial properties. They typically were embellished with elaborately decorated and brilliantly lit fronts to draw in customers. The nickelodeon showplaces were strictly designed for film, while the larger theaters continued, for a time at least, to concentrate on live entertainments.

As the public infatuation for the silver screen grew at a fantastic rate, grand motion picture theaters appeared in downtown business blocks. These movie palaces, embellished with lavish furnishings and elaborate stylistic elements, heightened the patron's sense of a world of fantasy. Dating largely from the 1910s and 1920s, these magnificent cinemas included the Clemmer in Spokane; the Paramount, Coliseum, and Fifth Avenue in Seattle; the Mount Baker in Bellingham; the Seventh Street in Hoquiam; and the Liberty in Walla Walla.

Hoquiam's Seventh Street Theater is a marvelous representative of this evolution in theater design. Although its Renaissance Revival exterior is quite handsome, it is the "atmospheric" interior that treats the patron's senses to a truly unique experience, simulating an evening under the stars in a Spanish village.

Hard times during the Great Depression drastically affected theater construction. Despite continued audience support, the structures built after the "Crash of '29" tended to be more modest in design.

Parks, Fairs, and Resorts

Arenas, grandstands, and related structures for county fairs, rodeos, and similar annual events are common throughout Washington, and many are historically important. In addition to state, county, and local sponsorship of fairs and events, Washington has hosted three world's fairs—two in Seattle (1909 and 1962) and one in Spokane (1974). Structures at these

**Wright Park
Conservatory**
Nestled near the
heart of downtown
Tacoma, this historic
late Victorian era
conservatory houses
hundreds of examples
of native and exotic
plants. The graceful
structure, built in 1907,
sits among towering
trees in Wright Park's
arboretum.
(National Register)

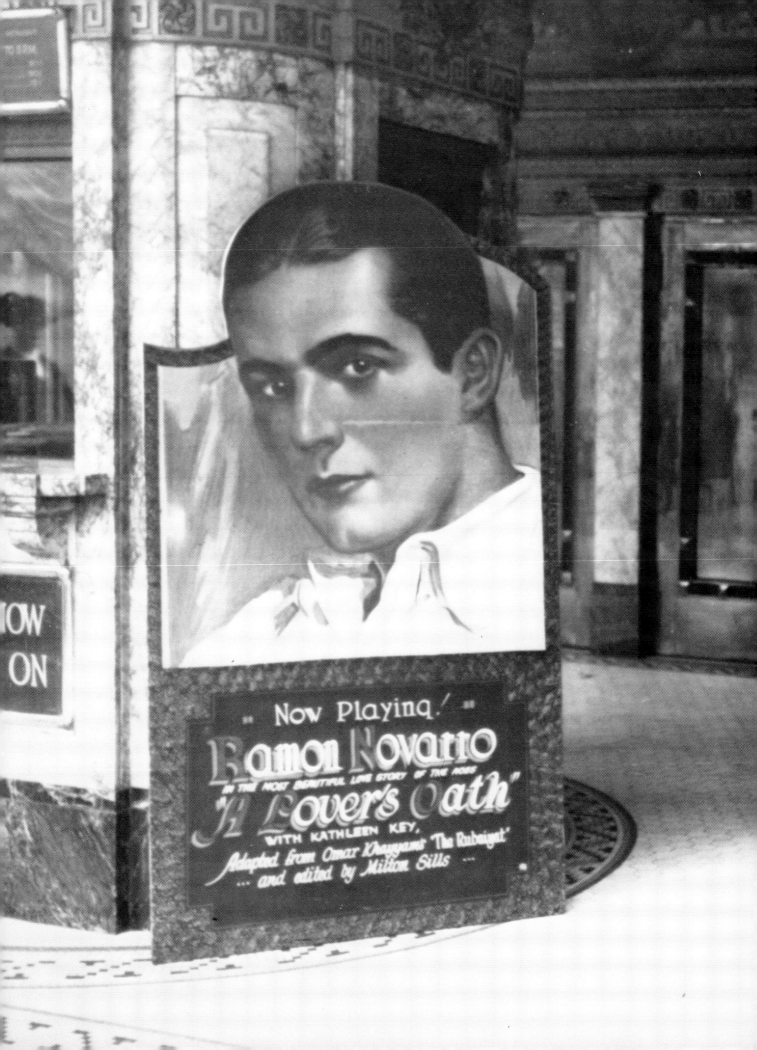

Now Playing!
Ramon Novarro
IN THE MOST BEAUTIFUL LOVE STORY OF THE AGES
A Lover's Oath
WITH KATHLEEN KEY.
Adapted from Omar Khayyam's "The Rubaiyat"
... and edited by Milton Sills ...

Pantages Theater

The Pantages Theater in downtown Tacoma was built during the height of the vaudeville era. Designed by B. Marcus Priteca for theater magnate Alexander Pantages, this magnificent structure was typical of the palatial era in American theater construction. Pantages embellished the theater interior with gold leaf and Renaissance ornamentation, sparkling chandeliers and light fixtures, murals and cornices, and elegant moldings. In the coved ceiling, a center glass panel inset with stained glass provided additional illumination. The entire effect achieved a fundamental purpose: to provide ordinary citizens with an escape from the mundane routine of their lives into a world of fantasy and opulence. (National Register)

Mineral Log Lodge
Built in 1906 on the
shores of Mineral Lake,
fifteen miles southwest
of Mount Rainier
National Park, the log
inn provided lodging for
skiers, hikers, and other
outdoor enthusiasts.
The logs were carefully
notched for precise fit
at the corners, and
narrow wedges of
wood were used for
chinking. Except for
the addition of modern
plumbing and
modernization of the
kitchen, the lodge
remains unaltered.
(National Register)

sites, most notably the Monorail and Space Needle at Seattle's 1962 World's Fair, and the United States Pavilion in Spokane, remain in use today.

Washington formerly boasted numerous amusement parks with picnic grounds, bandstands, ball fields, carnival attractions, concessions, and natatoriums (swimming areas, particularly indoor pools). Such facilities, accessible by city trolley lines, were a main recreational outlet for urbanites in the early twentieth century. These once popular entertainment complexes, however, have all but disappeared. With the proliferation of automobiles in the 1910s, new city and county park systems sprang up in outlying areas where motorists drove to picnic, play baseball, or swim.

Spokane's Natatorium Park, now long abandoned, was a noted amusement center standing next to the Spokane River. The famous Natatorium carousel, the only surviving structure from the site, is a rare and beautifully crafted merry-go-round constructed by Charles I. Looff. The carousel has been relocated in downtown Spokane at Riverfront Park where it remains in use today. An immensely popular attraction for children and adults alike, it is a vivid reminder of the kind of carefree entertainment indulged in by previous generations of Spokanites.

Conservatories likewise stood in many landscaped parks and playgrounds. Tacoma's Wright Park, established in the 1890s, was enhanced by the addition of a conservatory in 1907. This graceful, modestly-scaled structure consists of a central, multi-sided rotunda flanked by two wings. It occupies a site adjacent to an arboretum and small pond connected by meandering gravel paths. Residents of surrounding homes and apartments still utilize Wright Park today.

Bandstands, gazebos, and similar structures also were central attractions in many parks, and a number of them still remain in use. The Naches bandstand in Yakima County, for example, has been restored and relocated to its original location, and once again serves as a stage for concerts, speeches, and community dances. Causland Park in Anacortes has curving walls consisting of eccentrically patterned stonework and an oval shaped bandstand.

Horse racing remained an important form of recreation (and gambling) for Washingtonians throughout the nineteenth and into the twentieth century. In many of the early frontier communities roads served as local racecourses. Spokane's Altamont Boulevard, for example, originally was an old surrey track circling through the local countryside.

In the twentieth century, increasing numbers of sportsmen, mountain climbers, and other outdoor enthusiasts frequented wilderness resorts. The Mineral Log Lodge in Lewis County, for instance, served as a wilderness retreat for affluent residents from Tacoma and Seattle. The lodge appealed to vacationers looking for year-round recreation or the reputed therapeutic benefits of the mineral waters of that locality. A similar structure, standing in beautiful natural surroundings, is the Quinault Lodge in Grays Harbor County. Nestled among firs and cedars on the shore of Lake Quinault, this log and timber building and its ancillary structures have long served as a base for recreationalists visiting the Quinault area.

One exceptionally grand facility constructed to serve vacationers, mountaineers, and winter sports enthusiasts alike is Paradise Inn, located in Mount Rainier National Park. Completed in 1917, with an annex added in 1920, it stands near timberline on the slopes of Mount Rainier, and served as one of the earliest ski resorts in the nation. The original structure, composed of cedar logs, and the larger, shingled annex, were admirably designed to be compatible with the scenic subalpine landscape.

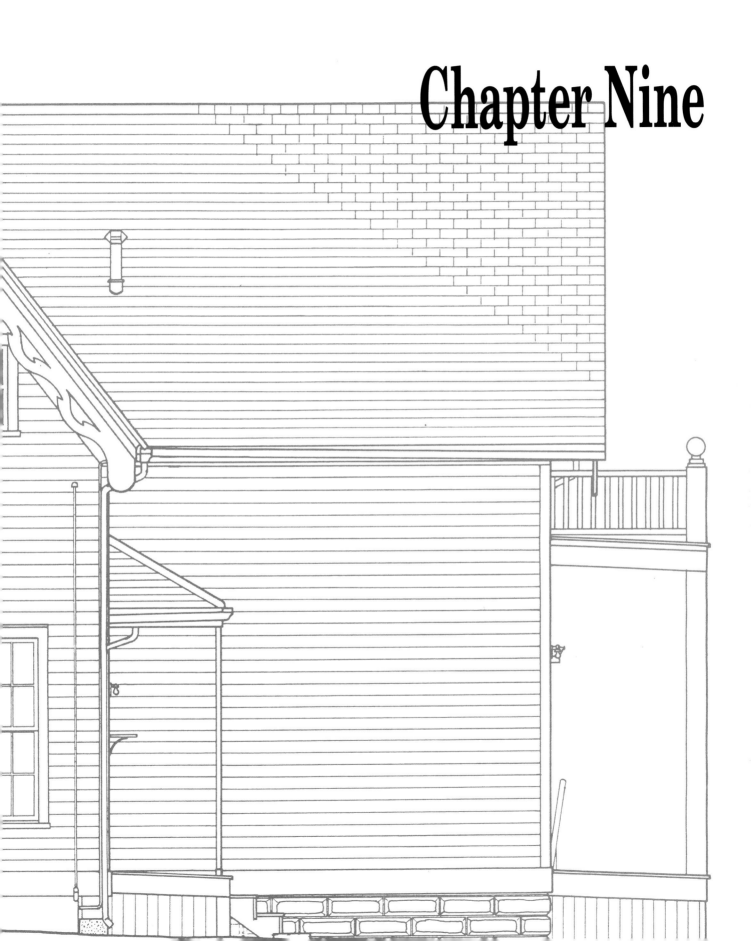

Chapter Nine

At Home in Washington

For the first American settlers, and for the thousands who followed them in the nineteenth century, the long and arduous journey to the Pacific Northwest was in large part a search for a home. The quest was rooted in the enduring Jeffersonian belief that America was a nation of yeoman farmers and independent homeowners, and the migration was fueled by the government's promise of generous land grants to individuals–up to 640 acres under the provisions of the Donation Land Law of 1850, and, a decade later, as much as 160 acres under the terms of the

Waikiki

The Spokane country estate of J. P. Graves reflects the appeal that architectural extravagance once had for Washington's nouveau riche. Designed by Kirtland Cutter, with interior by Elsie de Wolfe and landscape by the Olmsted brothers, the home was called "Waikiki" (spouting waters). Graves arrived in Spokane in the 1880s and was instrumental in the development of a streetcar line that later became the Spokane and Inland Empire Railroad. He also helped establish the city as a mining center. The original 1000 acre estate contained a wildlife sanctuary, brooks, ponds, and pasture for prizewinning cattle and sheep, as well as the English Tudor country manor. This photograph shows the formal garden with the tea house and surrounding decorative terraces. The estate also had an observatory, brick paths and walls throughout the grounds, farm buildings, and an ornate dolphin fountain. (National Register)

Bush Home
Among the first black pioneers to arrive in Washington, the Bush family settled near Tumwater and erected this home around 1878. A good example of single-wall box construction, the house was built of vertical cedar planks nailed to a sill at the bottom and a plate at the top. The arched window above the front entrance was typical of Gothic Revival architecture, a style common in the early years of Puget Sound settlement. The home is no longer standing. (Razed: State Inventory)

Homestead Act of 1862. But building a home on the frontier was beset with difficulties, due to the wilderness setting and the limited tools and materials available to settlers. In western Washington, in fact, some of the earliest homes were simply huts carved into the stumps of giant cedar trees, providing only the barest protection from the elements.

Far more common, of course, was the ubiquitous log cabin, built in all frontier areas before the widespread advent of sawmills and milled lumber. These small structures consisted of logs felled near the building site, then peeled and hewn, and notched at the ends. The logs were stacked horizontally one on top of another as closely as possible, and the spaces between were filled with chinking, usually mud and small pieces of wood, to form strong, weathertight walls.

Log cabins were well suited to a young democracy because such homes reflected few distinctions based on the status or wealth of the owner. In 1846, for example, Judge John R. Jackson fashioned his one room house near Marys Corner from rounded cedar logs; it was in this rustic cabin that he convened the first district court north of the Columbia River. Nearly twenty years later, stockmen along the Yakima River cut down cottonwood trees to build a similar structure known as the

Mattoon cabin, where they wintered before the spring cattle drives.

Some log structures were surprisingly substantial, such as the house that the Olmstead family built in 1875 on their ranch east of Ellensburg. Here, square-hewn cottonwood logs were carefully joined at the corners with dovetailed notches, reflecting the builders' skills with axe and adze. But typically, settlers considered log cabins to be temporary shelters, which would be abandoned for a frame house as soon as milled lumber became available.

Plank and Balloon Construction Techniques

In Washington, the wait usually was not long. When Captain Elijah H. McAlmond built the first frame house in Dungeness in 1867, a ripple of excitement swept through the community. "Houses were mostly built of logs," a neighbor recalled, but "when Captain McAlmond built one of real lumber throughout, actually lathed and plastered inside, with real boughten doors and a cornice around the roof, there was a general feeling that the county had taken a long stride toward the opulence and luxury of the old world."

The "long stride" in Dungeness was repeated again and again throughout Washington in the years before statehood. West of the Cascades, of

course, there was plentiful timber to supply an ever increasing number of sawmills. But lumber also became readily available in the treeless regions of eastern Washington, when timbermen cut lumber in the peripheral mountains and hauled it to the Columbia Plateau's agricultural communities.

During these years, age-old, hand-hewn construction methods were replaced by easier and more efficient techniques made possible by the output of building materials from sawmills. It

McAlmond House
The Elijah H. McAlmond house is all that remains of New Dungeness, one of the early settlements on the Olympic Peninsula. McAlmond was active in the coastal lumber trade and held several public offices. He was one of the first Clallam County commissioners. Ship carpenters built the house in the early 1860s from materials transported from Oregon. (National Register)

Perkins House
An outstanding example of the Italianate style, the Perkins house is urbane, sophisticated, and elegant. Built in 1885 by James Perkins, one of the founders of Colfax, the home copied the country houses of rural Italy, with projecting bays, ornate window treatments, and quoin embellished corners. The family's original log cabin home stands behind the house. (National Register)

was a period when the old and new often stood side by side—sometimes even interjoined in the same building. Some of the earliest frame houses incorporated hand-hewn timbers (usually sills and girders) along with machine-cut posts, studs, and clapboards from a nearby sawmill.

Pioneers also built simple "box houses," in which lumber planks were placed vertically, side by side, and nailed to a hand-hewn sill and plate. This cheap and expedient method of construction was used in the erection of some substantial and surprisingly stylish structures, such as Nathaniel Crosby's Gothic Revival cottage at Tumwater in 1858.

Although plank construction was promoted by some mid-nineteenth-century farm journals, another innovative method of construction—the "balloon frame"—soon dominated in Washington. The balloon frame, used as early as the 1830s in the Midwest, utilized lightweight lumber (usually 2" X 4" studs) fastened together with machine-cut nails. Compared to building with hand-hewn timbers joined by mortise and tenon, a balloon frame was easy to construct. In only a few days, several men could erect a frame home.

The first balloon frame houses in Washington were built by carpenters having no formal training in architec-

Lancaster House
This 1850 home located in Clark County is an excellent example of the Greek Revival style. The house is distinguished by a pedimented portico that shelters a two-story porch, and features classical moldings and Doric pillars and pilasters. (National Register)

tural design. Even so, these "vernacular" structures could be wonderfully evocative, reflecting styles once popular in areas of the East, Midwest, or South from which settlers had emigrated to the Pacific Northwest. As the years went by, these styles had passed out of fashion in the eastern United States, but remained popular on the relatively isolated Pacific coast. In the 1860s, Greek Revival houses such as David Rothschild's in Port Townsend (1868), with pedimented gables and corner

Goodwin Cabin

The first home for most pioneer settlers in nineteenth-century Washington was a hastily constructed cabin built from logs felled at the site. More often than not, these cabins were rudely built, temporary shelters soon replaced by more substantial frame houses when milled lumber became available. But not all log structures were so impermanent. The George Goodwin cabin built near Everson in Whatcom County was the home of a pioneer widely regarded for his expert skills with a broadax. Goodwin arrived in Everson in the 1870s and began cutting huge cedar trees and constructing numerous cabins. His own house is a particularly fine example of his craftsmanship. The one room cabin was built of massive cedar logs (each measuring eight-inches thick and up to thirty-two-inches high), hewn square, stacked horizontally, and joined at the corners by full dovetail notches (the strongest and most difficult notching technique). The logs were squared so precisely that no chinking was required to make the walls weathertight, and the dovetail notches gave the cabin maximum strength. Craftsmanship like this represented a kind of pinnacle for log construction and resulted in a sturdy home that outlasted less carefully built log structures—and many frame buildings too. (State Register)

Wells House

Arts and Crafts style influences are evident in the Wells house, built in 1909 in Wenatchee. Natural materials, including wood shingles and river rocks, were utilized to emphasize the hand-crafted features of this home. The house was built for W. T. Clark, known as the "father of the Wenatchee Valley" because of his role in creating an irrigation system that helped open the area to extensive orchard cultivation. (National Register)

pilasters, stood like primitive temples on the frontier, proclaiming an affinity with ancient Greek democracy. Others, built in the Gothic style, were frame versions of Andrew Jackson Downing's famous cottage designs.

Before long, however, balloon frame houses in a variety of up-to-date styles were being constructed across Washington. The increasing proliferation of manufactured building materials, the availability of pattern books, and the ever increasing population led to a building boom and a flowering of architectural styles. Whereas house design formerly evolved slowly over generations, builders now introduced new styles each decade or so.

By the 1880s, the finest homes in the territory had assumed a new sophistication, often reminiscent of the country villas of Italy with bracketed cornices, elaborate window hoods, and ornate bays. The 1890 Italianate mansion of Ezra Meeker in Puyallup, for example, was built by one of the territory's pre-eminent agriculturists and regional publicists. Not only did the facade attract attention, but the interior was richly outfitted with ornate fireplaces, ceiling frescoes, gold leaf moldings, stained glass, and other luxurious furnishings hardly imaginable a few years before.

The 1885 Italianate home of Colfax founder James Perkins was one of the grandest structures in the fertile Palouse country, as was William Kirkman's imposing brick Italianate mansion (ca. 1875) in prosperous Walla Walla. Whether in town or country, the message was clear: style had gained a foothold on the rough frontier.

Generally, however, Italianate style houses, like those from the earlier Greek and Gothic Revival period, were restrained when compared to the elaborate and diverse designs that burst forth on the scene after statehood in 1889. Earlier, builders had been subtly restricted by long held rules of symmetry and order, but designers in the

1890s felt no such constraints. Recognizing the inherent flexibility of the balloon frame, inspired by innovative designs, and financed by new found wealth, contractors now were free to be creative and extravagant.

The revolution in taste resulted in homes displaying strikingly irregular house plans and roof shapes, a wild variety of gables, towers, and bays, and a profusion of elaborate shingle banding and other ornamental woodwork. Internationally, it was the Victorian age; in Washington, the reign of the Queen Anne style.

In many ways, the Queen Anne style (and closely related forms such as the Stick and Shingle styles) reflected the brash and energetic character of the young state. It expressly utilized the endless variety of wooden sidings and ornamentation being turned out by the state's many sawmills. The result was a lively and elaborately textured facade.

Some houses, such as the home of contractor George Starrett (Port Townsend, 1889), reflected the explicit structural "honesty" of the Stick style idiom, in which decorative woodwork articulated the facade and suggested the frame beneath. Other examples, drawing upon the Shingle style variant, like the Saunders house (Port Townsend, 1891), were wrapped in a continuous covering of shingles, creating a taut and undulating surface.

In whatever mode, Queen Anne style houses provided an unparalleled opportunity for self-expression, allowing imaginative (if immodest) homeowners to display their artistic independence and unbridled success. In short, the Queen Anne style epitomized the notion that a man's home was his castle.

And, what castles they were! These were architectural designs that seemed to spread uncontrollably with turrets and towers, brackets and pendants, bargeboards and braces, great verandas and delicate cupolas. Every city boasted several outstanding examples, which invariably were the homes of prominent businessmen, entrepreneurs, and industrialists. Among the finest were the Gamwell and Louis White houses in Bellingham, the Gaches mansion in LaConner, the Roberts house of Spokane, the Lytle house or "Hoquiam's Castle" in Hoquiam, and Olympia's William White house. In the 1890s, entire suburban districts of Queen Anne houses were built in Spokane's exclusive Browne's Addition, on Seattle's First Hill, and along Eldridge Avenue in Bellingham. Even rural communities had treasured examples, such as the Hanford house outside Oakesdale or the Olsen house in Vader.

Less extravagant versions of the Queen Anne style home also were erected by the middle class. Many of these houses were built in standardized designs by tract developers, particularly in emerging streetcar suburbs, such as along South J Street in Tacoma where a row of Queen Anne homes still stand today. The Gilbert house in Yakima, on the other hand, was built by an individual homeowner using mail order construction plans. Even in its relatively modest form, the Queen Anne house displayed the ornamentation and variety of form and texture that were hallmarks of the style.

Workers' Cottages and Tenements

Domestic architectural trends at the turn of the century exhibited a darker side, too, underscoring deep class distinctions between the "haves" and "have-nots" in the industrial age. For every magnificent Queen Anne mansion built by a lumber baron, railroad tycoon, or mining capitalist, scores of workers' cottages were hastily and cheaply constructed. Most were small and simple—typically one-story frame structures, with hip or gable roofs and standing on barely adequate foundations. Workingmen's neighborhoods, such as Spokane's Pleasant Valley, stood near urban industrial and commercial districts. In small, company-owned lumber and mining towns, such as Black Diamond,

Roslyn, and Selleck, most of the homes in the community were laborers' quarters.

In larger communities, where the industrial economy attracted thousands of single men, scores of boardinghouses and cheap hotels were hastily erected in downtown districts such as Seattle's Chinatown, Belltown, and Pioneer Square. Typically, these structures packed dimly lit rooms down long central corridors. Rising as high as five stories, the living units were as crowded as the streets below or the factories and office towers standing nearby.

Not all working-class cottages were bleak domiciles, of course. Some diminutive Queen Anne cottages in mill towns displayed charm and domesticity. Nevertheless, as the twentieth century dawned, the houses of Washington's well-to-do stood in marked contrast to those of most workers.

Today, thousands of workers' cottages still are occupied, but, often as not, they are worn-out by the ravages of time. Consequently, entire urban neighborhoods of old workers' houses now are neglected and in dilapidated condition. Revitalizing these deteriorated turn-of-the-century housing tracts will be an important undertaking for future urban planners and developers.

Craftsman and Bungalow Designs

For the most part, the flamboyance of the Victorian era was muted after about 1905, as more harmonious forms and simplified ornamentation became popular. New styles ranged from the boxy Four Square, to the gabled English Cottage, to the stuccoed Mission Revival, to the prim Colonial Revival. In general, new homes were more modest and manageable than their Victorian antecedents.

Increasingly, in fact, the middle class shunned extravagance, while striving for simplicity, craftsmanship, and convenience in their homes. Plain surfaces, natural materials, open interior plans, and harmony with natural settings became evident in new house construction. At its best, the new suburban house served as a retreat from the clamor of the modern world, celebrating the notion of home as refuge in a machine-dominated age.

South J Street Historic District
This group of eight detached row houses is a good example of Queen Anne style structures built from "pattern book" designs. Constructed in 1889-1890 by the Washington Building Association of Tacoma, the homes are almost mirror images of each other. (National Register)

This desire for simplicity reflected the aesthetics of the Craftsman style. Architects derived their inspiration from the English Arts and Crafts movement, which had resurrected an almost medieval-like reverence for hand-made features and natural materials. Typical of the new style were the Wells house (Wenatchee, 1909), constructed of river rock and shingles, and the John Elston house (Aberdeen, ca. 1908), a skillful design incorporating board and batten siding and stick work.

The style was promoted by a small, but influential, group of professional architects. Perhaps the most notable was Ellsworth Storey who designed a number of houses in Seattle, including some cottages near Lake Washington in which the structural framework remained exposed on the exterior.

In eastern Washington, Kirtland Cutter designed romantically "rustic" cottages, such as his own Swiss chalet in Spokane and the shingled and stone cottage of industrialist Lewis Larson at Metaline Falls. The great Canadian Arts and Crafts architect, Samuel Maclure, built his only American residence at Ellensburg in 1905 for the David Ramsay family. It was typically Craftsman in appearance— a cottage with broad porches, an open interior, and handcrafted woodwork.

An entire suburban community built on the Arts and Crafts model was established near Medina on the east shore of Lake Washington. Conceived by architect/writer Alfred Renfro and cartoonist Frank Calvert, and funded by millionaire E. W. Johnston, Beaux Arts Village included small cottages in a wooded setting. A village commons, called Atelier Square, provided studios and work-shops for the artists who were expected to live in the tract.

The Craftsman movement, however, exerted its greatest impact with the introduction of the "bungalow" design in residential architecture. Tens of thousands of these efficient and attractive homes were built in town, city, and country. Mostly dating from the 1910s and 1920s, bungalows were inexpensive one-story structures with low-slung gable roofs, wide over-hanging eaves, and broad spacious porches, all exhibiting natural materials and simple, structural ornamentation.

The bungalow idiom, and the easy-going lifestyle that it was meant to enhance, were promoted by dozens of architectural books, magazines, and other publications. In fact, one of the nation's leading proponents was Seattle's Jud Yoho, whose *Bungalow Magazine* showed prototype designs used in countless new homes.

Mansions and Estates of the Nouveau Riche

While the middle class built homes exhibiting simplicity and practicality, the wealthy continued to spend enormous sums of money on lavish homes that sometimes rivaled the palatial estates of Europe's aristocracy. Ironically, the aggressive business titans who had shaped the modern industrial world were, at the same time, spellbound by the castles and country homes of earlier, more genteel times. In an eccentric way, this attitude was expressed at Medical Lake in 1900, when Lord Stanley Hallett built his baronial house. Hallett employed an entire family just to chip and shape the bricks used in construction so that the home would have a handcrafted appearance.

Although Washington's earliest mansions usually had been built near the heart of urban centers, industrial barons at the turn of the century began to move into exclusive suburban neighborhoods characterized by fine residential architecture, garden settings, curvilinear street plans, and panoramic views. The most famous of these elite districts included Browne's Addition and South Hill in Spokane, and First Hill and Capitol Hill in Seattle. But all of the larger communities had exclusive neighborhoods, including Grand Avenue and Rucker

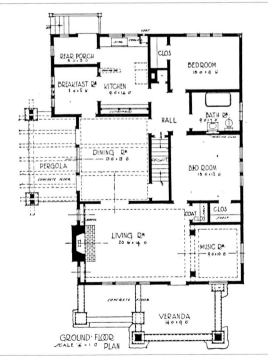

Seattle Bungalow
Bungalows provided inexpensive, comfortable housing for thousands of Washington families. This classic example, located in Seattle's Mount Baker neighborhood, was illustrated in *Bungalow Magazine,* in 1916 which provided readers with plans and specifications. (State Inventory)

Hoquiam's Castle
The use of an endless variety of wooden sidings and ornamentation in a lively and elaborate facade characterizes the home built by lumber baron Robert Lytle in Hoquiam in 1897. With its variously textured walls and roof forms, projecting bays and towers, and massive stonework base, the building conveys a sense of solidity and wealth. (National Register)

Hill in Everett, the Stadium-Seminary district in Tacoma, the Broadway district in Aberdeen, Nob Hill in Yakima, and Palouse Street in Walla Walla.

The wealthy who resided there valued the patina of age, and young professional architects gladly catered to their demands and indulged their fancies. Kirtland Cutter, for example, designed great English style country houses, such as Thornewood (Pierce County, 1909-1911), the James Graves estate (Spokane County, 1911), the Stimson-Green mansion (Seattle, 1899-1901), and the Glover mansion (Spokane, 1888). Cutter also designed imposing Neoclassical palaces, such as the Austin Corbin II house in Spokane. The lush, elaborate interiors of these great homes exhibited an even more eclectic range of periods and styles.

A long list of other regional architects worked in historic idioms as well: Herman Preusse and J. K. Dow of Spokane; Arthur Loveless, John Graham, James Schack, David Myers, Carl Gould, Charles Bebb, Leonard Mendel, and Joseph Cote in Seattle; Frederick Heath, and Babcock and Russell of Tacoma; and Joseph Wohleb in Olympia. They were joined, too, by nationally prominent architects, such as Charles Platt, who designed the Palladian-inspired Merrill house on Seattle's Capitol Hill in 1909-1910.

Architects did not work alone; they collaborated with interior designers (for example, Elsie de Wolfe), glass artists (such as Louis Comfort Tiffany), landscape designers (for instance, the Olmsted brothers), and woodcarvers and stonecutters. When a prominent Seattle resident, Eliza Ferry Leary, ordered the construction of the first great mansion (built 1901-1905) on the crest of Capitol Hill, she consulted with the Olmsteds, commissioned Tiffany, and employed Belgian woodcarvers for a year. Similar collaborative efforts where undertaken in the building of other prominent homes in Seattle, Spokane, Tacoma, and elsewhere.

By the 1910s, some of the state's wealthiest citizens moved beyond the city limits to establish secluded residential retreats, where imposing mansions stood in picturesque landscaped grounds. Seattle's Highlands community, designed by the Olmsted brothers, was a rolling, forested enclave located north of the city on a bluff overlooking Puget Sound. In this sylvan setting, William Boeing and other Seattle industrialists and financiers erected great estates. South of Tacoma, large houses with beautifully landscaped grounds (including Thornewood, designed by Kirtland Cutter) were built around several small lakes.

But the ultimate retreat was Sam Hill's country estate known as

Maryhill—a Renaissance palace designed by Washington, D. C., architects Hornblower and Marshall. Maryhill hauntingly stands atop a prominent butte in Klickitat County, overlooking the vast, treeless landscape of the Columbia River gorge in eastern Washington.

Suburbia and City

By the 1920s, Washington's middle class built its own diminutive versions of these mansions in suburban neighborhoods, resulting in neat rows of English cottages, Spanish haciendas, Colonial manors, and other houses built in so-called Period Revival styles. Homeowners randomly selected fanciful historical covers for otherwise ordinary homes.

Before the Great Depression, extensive suburbs stretched out from the urban core of every city. For the residents remaining behind, property became increasingly scarce and expensive. Not surprisingly, apartment houses, once condemned as immoral "French Flats" because of their close quarters, became respectable for small families, single men and women, and the elderly.

The finest apartments were outfitted in elegance despite their cramped size. They were draped in the familiar imagery of home or club, complete with maids' quarters, and spacious lobbies and grassy courtyards for the common use of the residents. The Tudor and Norman apartments of Fred Anhalt and the Spanish Colonial Revival apartments of Everett Beardsley in Seattle, as well as the Neoclassical and Renaissance Revival buildings of Albert Held in Spokane, were among the finest examples, attracting a clientele never before associated with apartment life.

Not all was ideal, of course. Too many workers—industrial wage earners, miners, immigrant laborers, and itinerant farmers—continued to live in shacks and tenements that mocked the notion of unlimited prosperity for all Americans. In the 1930s at the height of the Great Depression, Seattle's tent and cardboard shantytown, or "Hooverville," was one of the largest in the nation. It was a transient city-within-a-city, reflecting both the despair and the tenacious hope of the homeless.

Private home construction practically came to a halt during the Depression years and largely remained moribund until World War II. Consequently, when the war ended thousands of young families faced a housing shortage unrivalled in the state's history.

To address the crisis, the federal government subsidized the construction and purchase of new homes, and, at the same time, supported the building of low-income housing. One notable result was the construction of Seattle's Yesler Terrace project, begun in the early 1940s. It was a low density "garden community" that avoided the sullen institutional character of other housing projects around the country.

Meanwhile, a new school of residential architects emerged in Washington after World War II. The Northwest Style, practiced by architects like Paul Kirk, borrowed freely from several sources to create houses that were unmistakably modern, yet sensitive to tradition. Homes built in this style utilized low pitched gable roofs, the post and beam construction used by Native Americans, regional wood materials, and a careful consideration of siting to harmonize with nature. Such structures were as indigenous to the Pacific Northwest as the first log and plank houses of a century before. In post-war Washington, as on the frontier, home was more than simple shelter; it was a complex response to past traditions, present conditions, and future hopes.

Rust House
This Tacoma house, built in 1904 for industrialist William Ross Rust, is an excellent example of the Classical Revival style. This style drew upon the architectural elements of classical antiquity and the Renaissance. (National Register)

Washington Mutual Tower at 1201 Third Avenue / Wright Runstad & Company, Seattle

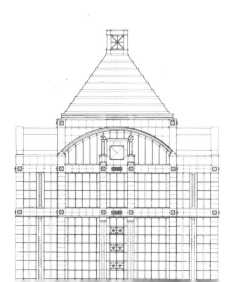

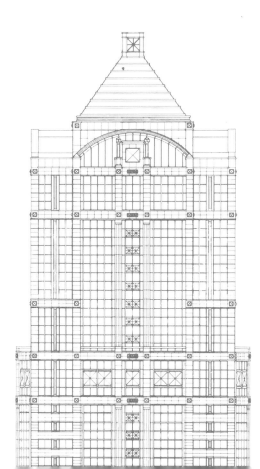

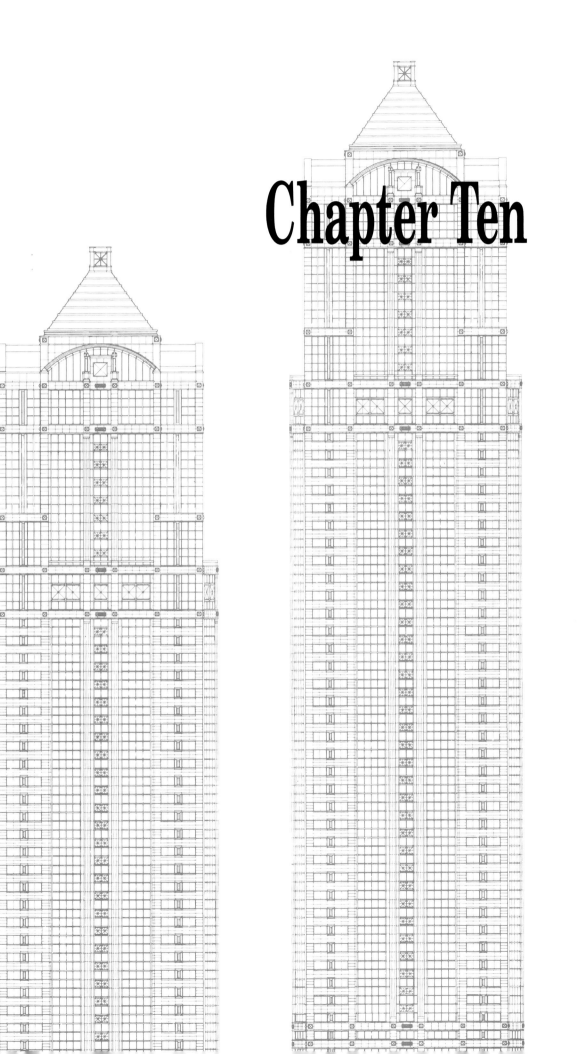

Chapter Ten

Space Needle
The 1962 World's Fair made Seattle the focus of international attention. With its theme "Century 21," the exposition looked boldly to the future. These preliminary drawings show the Space Needle, the Monorail, and the entrance to the United States Science Pavilion, and exemplify the visionary attitude that prevailed throughout the city, and, indeed, the state at that time. A dozen years later in Spokane, "Expo 74" reiterated that optimism, even as the country was thrust into an era of energy shortages and ecological problems. Expo, however, also made it clear that the benefits of modern technology must be tempered by an equal concern for the preservation of the environment.

Building for Tomorrow

During World War II, Washington experienced a tremendous increase in manufacturing as tens of thousands of laborers came to the region to join local workers in taking high paying jobs in shipyards, nuclear plants, aircraft factories, and other wartime industries. Most of the U. S. Navy's Pearl Harbor fleet was rebuilt in Northwest shipyards, and hundreds of new freighters and dozens of small aircraft carriers also came out of the docks. Airplane plants turned out bombers, while top secret nuclear facilities east of the Cascades produced plutonium for the first atomic bombs.

House by Thiry
Paul Thiry, one of the state's leading architects in the mid twentieth century, designed this house, illustrated in a special issue of *Architectural Record* in 1944. The design includes several features that distinguished his residential work, including post and beam construction, expansive glass walls, built-in storage units, and sliding doors. The interior and exterior surfaces are plastic-coated plywood, the latest in modern materials, but the heritage of the Northwest is evoked with a "Totem post" at the center of the facade.

Indeed, Washington's industrial workers, along with the region's farmers and lumbermen, played no small part in the war effort and the ultimate victory over the Axis powers. After the Japanese surrender, many of the wartime industries were converted to peacetime purposes, which remain important in Washington's economy today.

American aviation, in fact, had come of age in Washington in the years before the war. In Seattle, William Boeing had formed the nation's first great aviation conglomerate, which included not only the Boeing company, but also Pratt and Whitney, United Airlines, and other holdings. In the 1930s, government trustbusters broke the combine into its smaller components. But, with America's entry into World War II, the Boeing company was transformed into a major player in the national defense effort throughout the 1940s and beyond.

In recent decades, the corporation also has taken the lead in commercial aviation by pioneering the development of the modern jet airliner. Boeing has thrived with the phenomenal growth of the air travel industry, and today employs thousands of workers, engineers, and scientists. The vast size of the company's plants in the Puget Sound area reflects Boeing's scale of operations. Standing today at the

Everett facility, for example, is one of the largest manufacturing buildings in the world.

The rise of the nuclear industry was even more dramatic. After 1942, giant reactors and plutonium processors took shape at Hanford in the semiarid desert of central Washington. In this remote location, over 50,000 workers, including some of America's most brilliant scientists, toiled two years in secrecy to build the world's first full-scale plutonium factory. The structures at Hanford were the largest ever built by the DuPont company, and the sudden influx of workers led to the urbanization of the Tri-Cities practically overnight.

The most enduring legacy at Hanford is the B Reactor, which produced fissionable material for some of the first nuclear bombs. The facility remains today as a testament to the tremendous power unleashed in the atomic attack on Nagasaki at the end of the war. It is unquestionably a structure that helped shape the course of history. In the modern era, of course, Hanford also has turned to peaceful goals, conducting ongoing nuclear research and producing electrical energy.

Other industries, too, such as aluminum manufacturing and shipbuilding, thrived after the war, fueled by government contracts and cheap federally distributed electrical power. Aluminum smelters were established at Goldendale, Longview, Tacoma, and Spokane. In turn, these facilities provided aluminum for the shipyards at Bremerton, Vancouver, and elsewhere, and for the Boeing company plants on Puget Sound.

The development of these industries was dependent on a large federal presence in the state. Nowhere has this been more dramatically displayed than with the building of huge dams that tamed the Columbia and Snake rivers. Beginning during the Great Depression, the federal government financed the construction of a series of dams to provide for irrigation, navigation, flood control, and hydroelectric power. Private and local power companies also developed hydroelectric projects on the state's waterways.

Over the next four decades, fifteen major dams were built on the Columbia and Snake rivers alone. Meanwhile, the Bonneville Power Administration developed its "master grid," a network of transmission towers, high tension wires, and substations that distributed power throughout the region.

The largest dam was built at Grand Coulee on the Columbia River in north central Washington. When completed in 1941, it was the world's largest standing concrete structure.

Hanford B Reactor
The first full-scale plutonium reactor in the world was constructed at the Hanford Atomic Works in 1943-1944, and produced the plutonium used in the atomic bomb dropped on Nagasaki. In 1976, it was designated a National Historic Mechanical Engineering Landmark. A plaque at the site states: "This nuclear reactor was the first to demonstrate the practicality of producing large quantities of plutonium and was a major milestone in the United States Atomic Energy Program." (National Register eligible)

In addition to producing electricity and providing for flood control, Grand Coulee Dam diverted irrigation water for the Columbia Basin Project, which transformed great sections of central Washington's sagebrush-covered landscape into lush orchards and valuable cropland. Grand Coulee Dam's tremendous size and the vast scale of its technology were clear evidence of the growing power of man to harness nature.

Agricultural production and other extractive industries continued to expand after the war. Washington wheat and fruit were shipped throughout the nation and around the world. As new irrigation projects created arable land in central Washington, thousands of migrant workers (often from Mexico or the American Southwest) were hired to reap the rich fruit and vegetable harvests. Large cold storage structures and warehouses were built in Yakima, Wenatchee, and elsewhere to handle the produce before shipment to market.

Despite massive timber harvests earlier in the century, Washington still retained many of the last great stands of timber in the United States. Industrial giants, such as the Weyerhaeuser and Simpson companies, and many smaller firms continued to cut trees in substantial quantities. Sawmills and pulp mills produced lumber, paper products, siding, plywood, and other commercial products made from wood chips or other waste materials from the milling process. The industry also adopted scientific reforestation methods to preserve timber resources and to insure sustained yields.

Unlike the fly-by-night lumbermen of the early twentieth century, whose motto largely had been "cut it out, and get out," the modern wood products companies became well entrenched hometown businesses, establishing permanent sawmills, pulp mills, tree farms, laboratories, and headquarters in local communities. Weyerhaeuser's modern corporate headquarters, for example, designed by Skidmore, Owings, and Merrill in 1971, sits within a park-like, forested "campus" in Federal Way; the complex clearly indicates that the company is very much at home in Washington.

More than ever before, the products of the state's factories, fields, and forests were being sold in new markets abroad, particularly in Asia. Washington's ports, notably the container dock facilities at Tacoma and Seattle, had become important links in the Pacific Rim trading sphere.

The World's Fairs

Washington's new role on the national and international stage was fittingly acknowledged by the 1962 Seattle

Grand Coulee Dam

Grand Coulee Dam probably has had a greater impact on the state than any other single man-made structure. The effects of this project, the largest ever undertaken by the federal government up to that time, have been profound. The dam tamed the Northwest's mightiest river, and at the same time provided endless electrical power and diverted water that transformed great sections of semiarid desert into bountiful cropland.
(State Inventory)

World's Fair, an exposition taking as its theme "Century 21." Here, at a location just north of the city's downtown business district, rose a vision of a jet-age future, highlighted by the soaring Space Needle, the lacy arches of the United States Science Pavilion, and the Monorail. If this prophesy of a high-tech future was not entirely realistic, it was nonetheless an appropriate dream for a city and state whose best years seemed to lie ahead in a world of jet transportation and nuclear energy.

Spokane held its own international exposition twelve years later. Touted as an "environmental" fair, "Expo 74" was located next to the city's most significant natural feature, Spokane Falls. Ironically, the pavilions stood on the former site of the railroad yards that had done so much to mold the city into the economic and cultural center of the "Inland Empire." Futuristic technology was a theme at the fair, and the United States Pavilion, a giant modernistic structure, proved to be a central attraction. Of equal importance, however, was the new, growing awareness that our modern industrial society needed to develop a concern for ecological issues in order to protect the environment.

Despite the world's fairs, the most visible signs of growth in Washington in recent decades have not been space-age structures or speeding monorails, but rather rising skyscrapers, expanding suburbs, and proliferating roadways and interstate highways.

Today's Commercial District in City and Suburb

As elsewhere in America, the worst of the modern suburban sprawl led to endless strips of anonymous shopping centers, fast food franchises, and motels, with companion tracts of speculative housing. But Washington also had some of the nation's finest suburban landmarks.

Seattle's Lacey Murrow floating bridge was the largest of its kind in the world, when completed in 1940. This technological marvel spanned Lake Washington, opening Mercer Island and Bellevue to suburban development. Ten years later, the Northgate Shopping Center was built just north of Seattle. Designed by the John Graham architectural firm, the center included large department stores and small specialty shops situated around an open courtyard, all of which was surrounded by acres of parking. This formula soon was copied across America.

Less easily copied, but nevertheless influential, was the suburban residential architecture of the Northwest Style. Originating at a time when the standard "ranch house" design proliferated across America,

the Northwest Style homes were sited to take advantage of the natural setting, and featured post and beam construction and the wooden materials of the Pacific Northwest.

The gentle, human scale of these homes stood in marked contrast to the tall office towers rising in the larger cities. The most dramatic growth occurred in Bellevue, a former rural town that by the 1980s had grown into a new urban center east of Seattle. The central commercial district in the state's largest city had also grown taller and denser. In fact, Seattle's skyline in the 1980s was almost indistinguishable from that of other urban centers across the nation. The best of the new skyscrapers exhibited a stark, geometric beauty, such as the Seattle First National Bank Building (1969), a soaring rectangular tower of steel and glass standing at 1001 Fourth Avenue. Designed by corporate architectural firms, these buildings were elegant testimonials to the large-scale organizational capabilities of modern businesses.

**Northgate
Shopping Center**
One of the world's first regional shopping centers, Seattle's Northgate was a prototype that changed American shopping and living patterns. When construction was completed in 1950, it contained major department stores, specialty shops, and even a hospital and movie theatre, all within a single complex.

But, too often, city towers also bespoke a cold and impersonal quality that was the downside of the postwar building boom. The designs often shunned the livelier sculptural lines and rich ornamentation that were typical of an earlier generation of tall structures. At street level, few amenities accommodated pedestrians and the sheer size of the buildings created man-made canyons that overwhelmed, rather than inspired, the passerby. By the 1980s, however, architects began to break free of the "box" design to work with new forms—arched tops, curved walls, and setbacks—that at their best, as in the Washington Mutual Tower in Seattle at 1201 Third Avenue, evoked the sophistication, if not the controlled scale, of the Art Deco towers of the 1920s.

The Preservation Movement

The fast pace of change in the cities inspired a new concern for saving the best of the past. Seattle's preservation movement began in earnest in the early 1970s when voters created the Pioneer Square and Pike Place Market historic districts. Major preservation projects likewise arose in Spokane, Tacoma, Vancouver, and Yakima. The preservation movement caught hold in smaller towns too, especially those with largely intact historic commercial and residential districts, such as Port Townsend, LaConner, Snohomish, and Steilacoom. The movement has been active in eastern Washington as well—in Ellensburg, Colfax, Roslyn, Dayton, Waitsburg, Walla Walla, and on Main Street in Palouse.

In these and other communities across the state, residents recognize that whatever direction we take as a people, the buildings of the past will continue to enrich our present, and provide continuity and purpose as we move into the future.

Washington Mutual Tower

This high rise office building, constructed in the 1980s in downtown Seattle, exhibits a renewed interest in decorative forms and surfaces. With its sculpted roof lines, projecting and receding shapes, and varied colors, the Washington Mutual Tower contrasts with the simpler, darker box-like skyscrapers of the 1960s and 1970s.

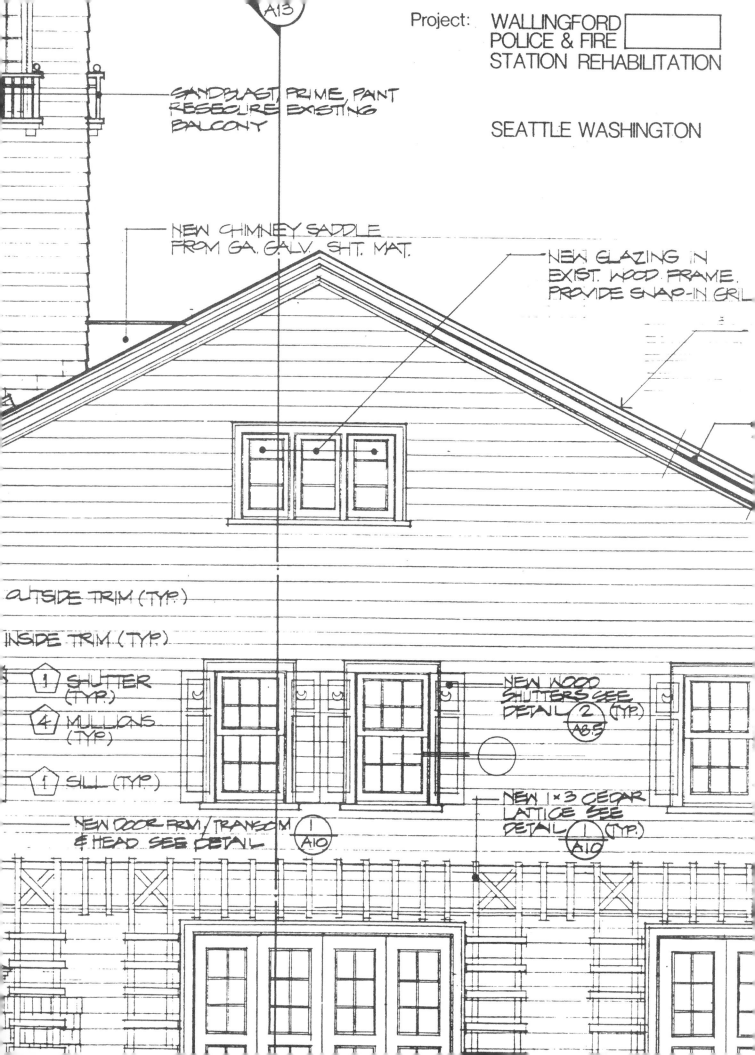

Project: WALLINGFORD
POLICE & FIRE
STATION REHABILITATION

SEATTLE WASHINGTON

SANDBLAST PRIME, PAINT
RESECURE EXISTING
BALCONY

NEW CHIMNEY SADDLE
FROM GA. GALV. SHT. MAT.

NEW GLAZING IN
EXIST. WOOD FRAME.
PROVIDE SNAP-IN GRIL

OUTSIDE TRIM (TYP.)

INSIDE TRIM (TYP.)

(1) SHUTTER
(TYP.)

(4) MULLIONS
(TYP.)

(1) SILL (TYP.)

NEW DOOR FRM/TRANSOM
& HEAD SEE DETAIL (1)/A10

NEW WOOD
SHUTTERS SEE
DETAIL (2)/A8.5 (TYP.)

NEW 1×3 CEDAR
LATTICE SEE
DETAIL (1)/A10 (TYP.)

Chapter Eleven

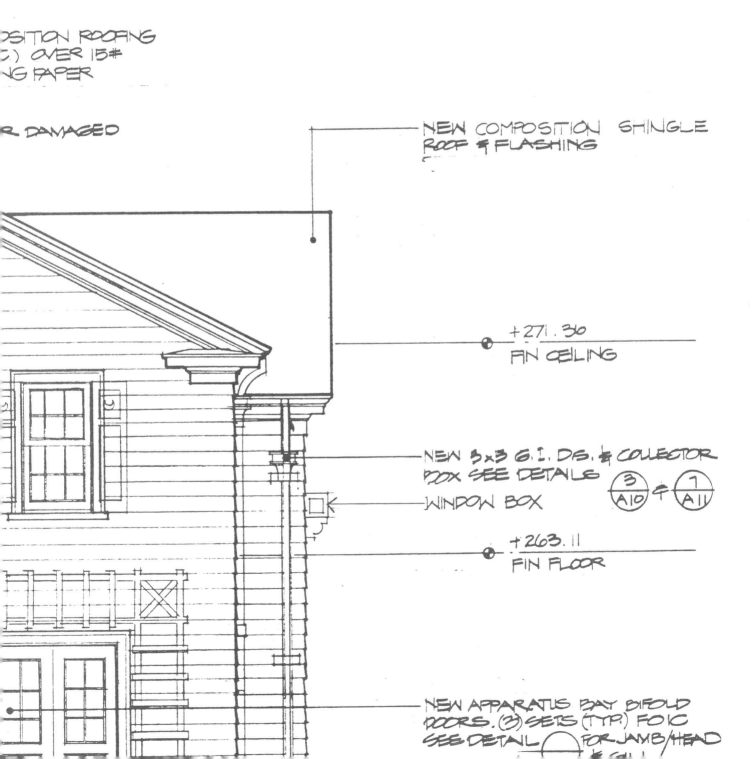

OSITION ROOFING
) OVER 15#
JG PAPER

R DAMAGED

NEW COMPOSITION SHINGLE
ROOF & FLASHING

+ 271.30
FIN CEILING

NEW 3×3 G.I. DS. & COLLECTOR
BOX SEE DETAILS ③/A10 & ⑦/A11
WINDOW BOX

+ 263.11
FIN FLOOR

NEW APPARATUS BAY BIFOLD
DOORS. (3) SETS (TYP.) FOIC
SEE DETAIL ⌒ FOR JAMB/HEAD

Epilogue

Until recently, preservation efforts in the United States mainly focused on protecting historic places that served to memorialize great events and people from the past. This concept now has given way to a broader sense of our heritage—one inspired by the belief that the future of our nation depends, in large part, on learning more about who we are and where we have been as a people.

Archaeologists have long viewed artifacts and other subsurface cultural features as a kind of prehistoric library. They reconstruct human history by analyzing the physical evidence of past cultures. The materials that they

Restoring the Will Jenne House
There are ongoing opportunities throughout Washington for persons to become involved in preservation projects. Here a painter helps in the restoration of the Will Jenne house on Whidbey Island. Built in 1890 in the Ebey's Landing area, this fine home was owned by the Jenne family for over sixty years. It now is included in the Central Whidbey Island Historic District, which is a collection of buildings and farmlands comprising a key part of Whidbey Island's National Historical Reserve. (National Register)

usually find to be most significant are the physical remnants from everyday life hundreds or thousands of years ago.

Today, the objectives of historic preservationists are often similar to those of the archaeologists. Preservationists, of course, still are concerned about protecting places associated with landmark events, major artistic efforts, and important persons, but they are equally interested in saving properties that depict the everyday experience of common people in past times.

Preservationists' efforts at protecting the "built" environment, particularly at the community level, have helped Washingtonians to better understand the past. A restored turn-of-the-century residential neighborhood, for instance, can tell us much about class structure and social life in the Victorian era. The Georgetown Steam Plant, dating from 1906, sat unnoticed for many years until researchers recently discovered its historical importance. It is the world's best remaining example of a type of technological facility that revolutionized electric power generation in the early twentieth century. While standing inside the structure, a visitor can see that the plant's designers were learning how to harness the vast amount of energy required to power a modern city.

A general understanding of history is a necessary part of everyone's education. According to state law, public school students must study American history. This requirement is based on the belief that history helps to teach common values, particularly an appreciation of our free society and its political traditions.

We also believe that a knowledge of history can help inspire a sense of social responsibility; students need to know about past mistakes in order to avoid repeating them when they assume leadership responsibilities as adults. Here again, historic preservation can make a contribution. For instance, a good way to reflect upon the injustice of the World War II internment of Japanese Americans, many of whom were U. S. citizens, is to visit the Puyallup Fairgrounds where they were illegally detained in 1942 and denied the due process of law.

In passing the National Historic Preservation Act of 1966, Congress intended to foster an understanding and appreciation of "heritage" for all Americans. The act expanded the National Register of Historic Places to include buildings and sites of state and local significance, as well as those of national importance. As a result, recognition now has been afforded to tens of thousands of historic and archaeological sites across the nation, and, together, these properties depict America's past in rich detail.

Washingtonians are increasingly concerned about protecting the natural environment, but they often remain unaware of continuing threats to the cultural or "built" environment. Few realize that more than half of the significant historic sites recorded statewide by the National Park Service in the 1930s no longer exist. The National Register of Historic Places has become something of an endangered species list for historic properties. Historic buildings are threatened by land development, fire, and neglect, and archaeological sites can by destroyed by artifact hunters, bottle collectors, erosion, and construction activity.

Public opinion surveys indicate that historic sites are popular visitor attractions; "heritage tourism" now is a major focus of the travel industry. In many communities, historic houses are in such demand by homeseekers that the prices they bring can exceed the cost of newly built residences. In cities and towns, millions of dollars have been invested in rehabilitating historic commercial districts under federal tax incentive programs, and, as a result, historic preservation has become a cornerstone of urban revitalization efforts.

There is always the risk that progress will be followed by complacency. Without ongoing maintenance, historic buildings can deteriorate to the point that they are no longer restorable. The need to preserve our national heritage will confront us in the future with the same persistence as the need to conserve clean air and water. It will be necessary for us to continually renew our efforts if we intend to save our historically significant buildings and sites for posterity.

Landes House

In the past two decades, Port Townsend has rediscovered its cultural and historic roots in its unique architecture. Encouraged by outside influences, the people of Port Townsend have responded with enthusiasm, energy, and pride in restoring many of the town's magnificent structures. Much credit for this awakening of community spirit can be given to Dr. William Murtaugh, Keeper of the National Register. On a visit to Port Townsend in 1975, Dr. Murtaugh said, "In the United States there are three great Victorian seaport communities: Galveston, Texas; Cape May, New Jersey; and Port Townsend, Washington." (Port Townsend Historic District, National Register and National Historic Landmark)

Selected Reading

Avery, Mary W. *Washington: A History of the Evergreen State.* Seattle: University of Washington Press, 1975.

Buerge, David M., and Junius Rochester. *Roots and Branches: The Religious Heritage of Washington State.* Seattle: The Church Council of Greater Seattle, 1988.

Calvert, Frank, ed. *Homes and Gardens of the Pacific Coast. 1913;* rpt. Seattle: Allied Arts, 1974.

Clark, Norman H. *Washington: A Bicentennial History.* New York: W. W. Norton, 1976.

Faber, Jim. *Steamer's Wake.* Seattle: Enetai Press, 1985.

Ficken, Robert, and Charles LeWarne. *Washington: A Centennial History.* Seattle: University of Washington Press, 1988.

Gilliford, Andrew. *America's Country Schools.* Washington, D. C.: Preservation Press, 1984.

Hill, Beth, and Ray Hill. *Indian Petroglyphs of the Pacific Northwest.* Seattle: University of Washington Press, 1974.

Jackson, W. Turrentine. *Wagon Roads West: A Study of Federal Road Surveys and Construction in the Trans-Mississippi West (1846-1869).* Lincoln: University of Nebraska Press, 1979.

Johnston, Norman J. *Washington's Audacious State Capitol and Its Buildings.* Seattle: University of Washington Press, 1988.

Kauffman, Henry J. *The American Farmhouse.* New York: Hawthorn, 1975.

Klamkin, Charles. *Barns: Their History, Preservation, and Restoration.* New York: Hawthorne, 1973.

Kline, Mary S., and G. A. Bayless. *Ferryboats: A Legend on Puget Sound.* Seattle: Bayless Books, 1983.

Kreisman, Larry. *Apartments by Anhalt.* Seattle: Office of Urban Conservation, 1978.

Kreisman, Lawrence. *Art Deco Seattle.* Seattle: University of Washington Press, 1980.

———. *Historic Preservation in Seattle.* Seattle: Historic Seattle Preservation and Development Authority, 1985.

McGregor, Alexander Campbell. *Counting Sheep: From Open Range to Agribusiness on the Columbia Plateau.* Seattle: University of Washington Press, 1982.

Meinig, D. W. *The Great Columbia Plain: A Historical Geography, 1805-1910.* Seattle: University of Washington Press, 1968.

Mills, Randall V. *Stern-wheelers Up Columbia: A Century of Steamboating in the Oregon Country.* Palo Alto: Pacific Books, 1947.

Morgan, Murray. *Puget's Sound: A Narrative of Early Tacoma and the Southern Sound.* Seattle: University of Washington Press, 1979.

———. *Skid Road: An Informal Portrait of Seattle.* Seattle: University of Washington Press, 1982.

Nabakov, Peter, and Robert Easton. *Native American Architecture.* New York: Oxford University Press, 1989.

Naylor, David. *American Picture Places: The Architecture of Fantasy.* New York: Van Nostrand Reinhold, 1981.

Newell, Gordon R. *Ships and the Inland Sea: The Story of the Puget Sound Steamboats.* Portland: Binfords and Mort, 1960.

Pearson, Arnold. *Early Churches of Washington State.* Seattle: Allied Arts of Seattle, 1979.

Sale, Roger. *Seattle, Past to Present.* Seattle: University of Washington Press, 1976.

Scott, James W., and Roland L. DeLorme. *Historical Atlas of Washington.* Norman: University of Oklahoma Press, 1986.

Shideler, James H. *Agriculture in the Development of the Far West.* Goleta, California: Kimberly Press, 1975.

Skallen, Michael. *The Ferry Story: The Evergreen Fleet in Profile.* Seattle: Superior Publishing, 1983.

Stewart, Hilary. *Cedar: Tree of Life to the Northwest Coast Indians.* Seattle: University of Washington Press, 1984.

———. *Indian Artifacts of the Northwest Coast.* Seattle: University of Washington Press, 1975.

Vaughn, Thomas, and Virginia Guest Ferriday, eds. *Space, Style, and Structure: Building in Northwest America.* 2 vols. Portland: Oregon Historical Society, 1974.

Woodbridge, Sally B., and Roger Montgomery. *A Guide to Architecture in Washington State: An Environmental Perspective.* Seattle: University of Washington Press, 1980.

Wright, E. W., Ed. *Lewis and Dryden's Marine History of the Pacific Northwest.* New York: Antiquarian Press, 1961.

Photographic Credits

Each chapter in this book is illustrated with historic and contemporary photographs of properties from the files of the Office of Archaeology and Historic Preservation. Most of the properties are listed in the National Register and State Register of Historic Places or the State Inventory, and currently are standing. While there may be thousands of sites suitable for each chapter theme, the properties shown here were selected for outstanding architectural merit, historic significance, integrity, or as unique examples of preservation. The following list is provided for additional research and contains locational information, photographer's name and date of photograph if known, image or negative number, and source.

WASHINGTON'S FIRST BUILDERS
Sweathouse - Asahel Curtis, 1915, Curtis Collection (Image #33444), Washington State Historical Society

Stratigraphy - Sketch by Robert Whitlam, 1989, Washington State Office of Archaeology and Historic Preservation

Rock Alignment - Robert Whitlam, 1988, Washington State Office of Archaeology and Historic Preservation

Storage Pit - Robert Whitlam, 1988, Washington State Office of Archaeology and Historic Preservation

Indian Boys Building a House - Samuel Morse, circa 1889, Morse Collection (Image #465), Washington State Historical Society

Mat Lodge - Edward S. Curtis, circa 1910, Special Collections Division (Negative No.: NA13), University of Washington

Indian Fort - Joseph Drayton, circa 1841 (Negative number OrHi 46195), Oregon Historical Society

Peeled Cedar Tree - Rick McClure, 1982, Gifford Pinchot National Forest
Ozette Village - Photographer unknown, circa 1917, (Image #IND/MAK 3.03.001), Washington State Historical Society

BUILDINGS OF THE EARLY FRONTIER

Crockett Blockhouse - Bob Larsen, 1971, Washington State Office of Archaeology and Historic Preservation
Grant House - Stephen Mathison, 1984, Washington State Office of Archaeology and Historic Preservation
Nathaniel Orr Home - Steve Fischer, 1989, Town of Steilacoom
Fort Nisqually - C. A. Darmer, circa 1880's, Special Collections Division (Negative No.: UW Neg 1802a), University of Washington
Olmstead Place - Photomaps, 1960, Washington State Office of Archaeology and Historic Preservation
Commandant's Quarters at Fort Simcoe - Photographer unknown, 1971, Washington State Office of Archaeology and Historic Preservation
Joseph Borst Home - Florence Lentz, 1977, Washington State Office of Archaeology and Historic Preservation

BOUNTIFUL HARVESTS

Marble Ranch Round Barn - 2G Design, 1986, Washington State Office of Archaeology and Historic Preservation
Jacob Ebey House - Bob Larsen, 1971, Washington State Office of Archaeology and Historic Preservation
LaFramboise Property - Sara Steel, 1985, Washington State Office of Archaeology and Historic Preservation
Max Steinke Round Barn - Craig Holstine, 1988, Washington State Office of Archaeology and Historic Preservation
Ebey's Landing - Photographer unknown, circa 1900, Trust Board of Ebey's Landing National Historical Reserve
Interior Grain Tramway - Craig Holstine and Glen Lindeman, 1988, Washington State Office of Archaeology and Historic Preservation
Woolrey-Koehler Hop Kiln - Mark Brack, 1983, Washington State Office of Archaeology and Historic Preservation
Sawyer House - Florence Lentz, 1976, Washington State Office of Archaeology and Historic Preservation
Saturno-Breen Truck Farm - Stephen Mathison, 1980, Washington State Office of Archaeology and Historic Preservation

TRAILS, SHIPS, AND RAILS

Ferryboat on Puget Sound - Joe Williamson, 1948, Mukilteo Maritime Ferryboat Museum
Corduroy Road - Photographer unknown, 1984, Western Heritage, Inc.
Devil's Walkway - Jet Lowe, 1989, HAER, National Park Service
Curtis Wharf - Peter T. Donahue, circa 1987, Washington State Office of Archaeology and Historic Preservation

Grays River Covered Bridge - Photographer unknown, 1962, Washington State Office of Archaeology and Historic Preservation

Sehome Wharf - Photographer unknown, 1892, Buswell Collection, Center for Pacific Northwest Studies

Yakima Valley Transportation Company - Photographer unknown, 1983, Washington State Office of Archaeology and Historic Preservation

Schooner Wawona - Photographer unknown, date unknown, Williamson Collection, Puget Sound Maritime Historical Society

Liberty Stage Office - Jacob Thomas, 1974, Washington State Office of Archaeology and Historic Preservation

Union Station - Photographer unknown, circa 1975, Department of Community Development, City of Tacoma

FACTORIES, MINES, AND MILLS

Dickman Headsaw - Photographer unknown, circa 1979, Washington State Office of Archaeology and Historic Preservation

F. Arnold Polson House - Stephen Mathison, 1979, Washington State Office of Archaeology and Historic Preservation

Tenino Stone Quarry - Photographer unknown, circa 1895, *The Tenino Independent*

Roslyn Historic District - Florence Lentz, 1976, Washington State Office of Archaeology and Historic Preservation

Thorp Grist Mill - Florence Lentz, 1976, Washington State Office of Archaeology and Historic Preservation

Beehive Ovens - Photographer unknown, circa 1901, Robert Teagle private collection

Electron Flume - Photographer unknown, 1910, Puget Sound Power and Light Company Collection (# 358), Special Collections Division, University of Washington

Snoqualmie Falls Generating Station - Photographer unknown, circa 1975, Puget Sound Power and Light Company

Chinese Walls - Lisa Soderberg, circa 1979, Washington State Office of Archaeology and Historic Preservation

Irondale Housing - Lisa Soderberg, 1983, Washington State Office of Archaeology and Historic Preservation

Georgetown Steam Plant - Jacob Thomas, 1977, Washington State Office of Archaeology and Historic Preservation

MERCHANTS ON MAIN STREET

Riverside Avenue - Photographer unknown, circa 1920 (Negative No.: UW 9029), Special Collections Division, University of Washington

Oxford Tavern - Dan Bothell, 1989, Washington State Office of Archaeology and Historic Preservation

Port Townsend Business Block - Jacob Thomas, 1975, Washington State Office of Archaeology and Historic Preservation

Starbuck Bank - Florence Lentz, 1977, Washington State Office of Archaeology and Historic Preservation

Smith Tower - Photographer unknown, circa 1914, Special Collections Division (Negative No.: UW Neg 388), University of Washington

Cloverland Garage - Photographer unknown, circa 1918, Washington State Office of Archaeology and Historic Preservation

Tacoma Warehouse District - Christopher Steel, 1989, Washington State Office of Archaeology and Historic Preservation

Davenport Hotel - Photographer unknown, circa 1975, Washington State Office of Archaeology and Historic Preservation

Northern Life Tower - Jacob Thomas, 1975, Washington State Office of Archaeology and Historic Preservation

Teapot Dome - Leonard Garfield, 1985, Washington State Office of Archaeology and Historic Preservation

FOUNDATIONS OF THE COMMUNITY

Holy Trinity Orthodox Church - Kelly McGrew, 1989, Washington State Office of Archaeology and Historic Preservation

Garfield County Courthouse - Stephen Mathison, 1979, Washington State Office of Archaeology and Historic Preservation

Wallingford Fire Station - Stephen Mathison, 1984, Washington State Office of Archaeology and Historic Preservation

Blue Mountain School - Photographer unknown, 1908, Washington State Office of Archaeology and Historic Preservation

Japanese Language School - Marvin Boland, circa 1927, (Image #E2717) Washington State Historical Society

Claquato Church - Douglas Whisman, 1973, Washington State Office of Archaeology and Historic Preservation

Slavonian Hall - Christopher Steel, 1989, Washington State Office of Archaeology and Historic Preservation

Masonic Temple - Jacob Thomas, 1975, Washington State Office of Archaeology and Historic Preservation

Redman Lodge - Jacob Thomas, 1975, Washington State Office of Archaeology and Historic Preservation

WASHINGTON AT PLAY

Natatorium Carousel - Sally Reynolds, 1989, Washington State Office of Archaeology and Historic Preservation

Capitol Theater - Stephen Mathison, 1979, Washington State Office of Archaeology and Historic Preservation

Naches Bandstand - Jack Dodge, 1986, Washington State Office of Archaeology and Historic Preservation

Wright Park Conservatory - Florence Lentz, 1976, Washington State Office of Archaeology and Historic Preservation

Pantages Theater - Photographer unknown, date unknown, Tacoma Public Library

Mineral Log Lodge - Jacob Thomas, circa 1973, Washington State Office of Archaeology and Historic Preservation

AT HOME IN WASHINGTON

Waikiki - Photographer unknown, 1912, Cutter Collection, Eastern Washington State Historical Society

Bush Home - Walter T. Vitous, 1969, Washington State Office of Archaeology and Historic Preservation

McAlmond House - James Vandermeer, 1981, Washington State Office of Archaeology and Historic Preservation

Lancaster House - Jacob Thomas, 1974, Washington State Office of Archaeology and Historic Preservation

Perkins House - Jacob Thomas, 1976, Washington State Office of Archaeology and Historic Preservation

Goodwin Cabin - Photographer unknown, 1880, Center for Pacific Northwest Studies, Western Washington University

Wells House - Photographer unknown, circa 1972, Washington State Office of Archaeology and Historic Preservation

South J Street Historic District - Mark Brack, 1985, Washington State Office of Archaeology and Historic Preservation

Seattle Bungalow - Leonard Garfield, 1989, Washington State Office of Archaeology and Historic Preservation

Floor Plan - Architect unknown, 1916, *Bungalow Magazine*

Hoquiam's Castle - Jacob Thomas, 1976, Washington State Office of Archaeology and Historic Preservation

Rust House - Caroline Gallacci, 1985, Washington State Office of Archaeology and Historic Preservation

BUILDING FOR TOMORROW

Space Needle - Yang Color Photography, circa 1962, Special Collections Division (Negative No.: UW Neg 10114), University of Washington

House by Thiry - Illustrator unknown, 1944, *Architectural Record*

Hanford B Reactor - Photographer unknown, 1944 (Photo No. 90244-5), U.S. Department of Energy

Grand Coulee Dam - Bureau of Reclamation, circa 1940, Northwest Room, Washington State Library

Northgate Shopping Center - Photographer unknown, 1950, Northgate Shopping Center

Washington Mutual Tower - Photographer unknown, 1989, Wright Runstead and Co.

EPILOGUE

Jefferson School Demolition - Brad Garrison, 1985, *West Seattle Herald*

Restoring the Will Jenne House - Stephen Mathison, 1984, Washington State Office of Archaeology and Historic Preservation

Landes House - Stephen Mathison, 1984, Washington State Office of Archaeology and Historic Preservation